I have much gratitude for my partner Linda Batina Solomon sharing her wonderful painting of the Whirling Dervishes on the cover of this book. This art piece is on the wall in my office. Batina and I are both blessed to be connected to these Dervishes. We share with many others around the world, the Dances of Universal Peace, once called Sufi Dancing. The Dances of Universal Peace, as do all Sufi's, have one intention, to bring Love, Peace and Harmony to our world.

# Sharing Life
## with Another

*A Memoir of a Social Worker*

Poignant End of Life Stories

Bob Sh'mal Ellenberg

**BALBOA**
PRESS

A DIVISION OF HAY HOUSE

Balboa Press books may be ordered through booksellers or by contacting:

Balboa Press
A Division of Hay House
1663 Liberty Drive
Bloomington, IN 47403
www.balboapress.com
1 (877) 407-4847

Because of the dynamic nature of the Internet, any web addresses or
links contained in this book may have changed since publication and
may no longer be valid. The views expressed in this work are solely those
of the author and do not necessarily reflect the views of the publisher,
and the publisher hereby disclaims any responsibility for them.

The author of this book does not dispense medical advice or prescribe the use
of any technique as a form of treatment for physical, emotional, or medical
problems without the advice of a physician, either directly or indirectly. The
intent of the author is only to offer information of a general nature to help
you in your quest for emotional and spiritual well-being. In the event you use
any of the information in this book for yourself, which is your constitutional
right, the author and the publisher assume no responsibility for your actions.

Any people depicted in stock imagery provided by Thinkstock are
models, and such images are being used for illustrative purposes only.
Certain stock imagery © Thinkstock.

Printed in the United States of America.

ISBN: 978-1-4525-9373-9 (sc)
ISBN: 978-1-4525-9374-6 (e)

Balboa Press rev. date: 04/30/2014

Cover painting by Linda Solomon

# Contents

# Mom – You Have to Eat

When my 84 year-old Mother was in the hospital for two weeks unable to eat and her doctor not knowing how to help, at some point I felt it was my job to do something. Unlike most people I don't consider the medical profession the first, last and only word on how to care for someone. It was never my way to abrogate my children's care or my own to others, so I felt compelled to do what I could for my mother.

Mom was admitted to the hospital with two cracked ribs. This happened when she was about to come out of the elevator in the retirement building where she lived. Somehow when the door opened she was thrust forward causing her body to be thrown out the door? Mom landed against a chair in the lobby. The shock, I suppose, caused her to have a slight cardiac failure. The doctor assured me that both problems could be treated easily. She didn't appear to be in any medical crisis and we hopefully expected her to be discharged soon. This thinking changed quickly.

After being in the hospital for a couple of days, Mom

complained about a bad taste in her mouth. This made her whole face scrunch up with every bite of food she took. The taste felt so bad she couldn't keep any food in her mouth. She could only describe the sensation as "Feeling like sandpaper." Mom was admitted weighing only 93 pounds so there wasn't much leeway for her to lose weight.

Naturally the hospital staff and I thought it would pass. When after a few days it didn't pass I called my sister, Tina, asking her to come down to Florida from New York to help me get our Mom to eat. For two weeks, my sister, each of our daughters, the nurses and I cajoled, pleaded and explained to her she was getting weaker and weaker. We all had the same mantra: "You have to begin eating." She understood; she didn't have dementia and was aware of what was going on. "I want to eat Robert," she said weakly. "You know I love food. What can I do? Pickles, pizza, steak, pastrami, fruit. I want everything, but something is wrong. Nothing tastes right. I don't want to die; I want to go to the movies, the mall. I want to dance, go out to eat. Everything: I want do everything I love. Please have the doctor do something."

It was an impassioned plea for help, but the doctor didn't have a clue what to do. Working as a medical social worker in a nursing home I believed I knew how some doctors felt about elder patients: They are ready to give them up. My Mother's doctor was no help. He was never able or even suggested a diagnosis for her mouth problem. When I suggested to him that maybe some digestive juices were coming into her mouth from the injury, he simply discounted my idea. There was no choice: I discussed it with my sister and Mom agreed; since the medical people weren't doing anything I would take her home to her apartment. I had the hope that with my lady friend, Klaudyna, myself, and with her good friends at the retirement building, she would be encouraged to eat.

It was the week of Chanukah and Christmas. This made me feel positive and encouraged. Although we are Jewish, my mother was never much for religious observance, but to me, it felt like a good time for healing. Klaudyna, a young Catholic woman from Poland, helped set up a Christmas table in the living room. Then together we created a Chanukah table in Mom's bedroom, along with a colorful "Happy Chanukah" banner on the wall. We tried to make it as joyous as possible. Unfortunately when Mom came home she was focused only on her bed. She immediately, with some help from me, climbed into it, not noticing our efforts to perk her up. I pointed out the "Happy Chanukah" banner and colorful table with a menorah (a ritual Chanukah candelabra) the candles, flowers and the get-well cards. Mom only gave a faint smile and turned away. Normally my mother would appreciate and be so thankful for these extras on her behalf. I accepted her lack of interest due to her condition, and now, there was some depression.

With some uncertainty about what was going to happen, and what we were going to do; Klaudyna and I put a mattress on the living room floor. We planned to do all we could to help my Mother regain her strength.

Her first night home was the third night of Chanukah. When we lit the candles I made extra special prayers that the sacred light of the holiday candles would spread healing energy to my mother. On each of the following five nights, I made a special prayer for "The light of the candles to bring my mother comfort and strength."

When her friends heard she was home, they made a parade of visits to her bedside. Each in turn encouraged her to eat and get stronger. But these elders all came out of her room despondent, seeing how weak and debilitated she had become. They couldn't find her bright smile and good cheer that was gone from her face. One of her dearest friends, Dotty, came in with some Christmas chocolate. She hoped the sweet taste would be a turning point. The two of them were sweetaholic partners. Dotty didn't want to lose her. Dotty came up to Mom's bed and said, "Mae, you have to begin someplace; here's what you love." I was standing in the doorway watching, and was surprised when mom actually turned her face away. But Dotty, a feisty woman of 93, persisted until Mom turned her face to Dotty, who then put the chocolate directly into her friend's mouth. Mom sucked on the chocolate for few seconds, before she pushed it through her dried lips with her tongue. She had the same scrunched up look on her face. "I'm sorry Dotty, I can't eat it," she murmured. It was hard to fathom my mother being unable to dissolve the sweetness in her mouth. It made no difference. Her male friend, John, came by everyday to encourage her, but also left uncertain. It was depressing to everyone who came to see her slowly withering away.

After a few days in her apartment, the question was in my mind if anything was going to reverse her crisis. She was still barely eating or drinking. Only getting weaker. Yet in a raspy, whisper, "Robert, you know I love life, I don't want to die." I assured her, "Mom, you're not going to die, but you have to eat." I said the words, but knew she was getting close to death.

One or two times during the night, she would cry out to me in a long, drawn out, weak voice, "Rah-ah-bert." I would get up and help her out of bed. Then we walked very slowly, with her literally hanging onto me, my arm around her waist, taking her to the bathroom. There, she would take her time urinating with her weakened torso and head down, low to her thighs. (We had a potty chair right next to her bed, but because of pride, even under this circumstance, she refused to use it.) It was sad and heartbreaking for me to see my Mother so weakened, unable to enjoy life, which on some level gave her so much pleasure.

One thing that did turn her on was ice. She didn't want the ice to suck on, but to rub around her lips, chin, and cheeks. Initially, Klaudyna or I brought ice for her to suck on, and wet her mouth, but very quickly it became something else. During the day and at night, time and again, all she wanted was ice. She would take my hand, or using her own, move the ice all over her face. As I sat, during one nighttime vigil, watching over her, a realization came to me: There was something about what she was doing that looked ... sensuous. "Don't be weird, Bob," I thought to myself, watching the repetitive action of this old lady, my mother, rubbing ice all over her face and I'm thinking sensuality. During another middle of the night vigil, I again brought her ice chips. I sat looking at her rubbing the ice over her bony, narrow, pale, face, and she whispered, " Robert, it's strange, but it feels sexy." Good ole mom. Sexy??? Was it my thought she picked-up;

her thought I received, or was something else going on? Here my Mother was on what might be her deathbed, her last days, saying rubbing ice on her face was sexy. One afternoon she actually told Dotty the ice was keeping her alive. Ice chips rubbed on face—sexual ideation—equal life. Go figure.

Naturally we never stopped offering her food and drink: tea, milk, oranges, lemonade, water, nutritional supplements with ice cream, banana, and oatmeal. We brought her whatever she asked for but all she could take was a sip, a bite, nothing to sustain her life.

What she also enjoyed was my light, gentle massage, to her feet, her hands and especially her back. Reaching a hand around her back, she'd take my hand and hold it firmly in certain places. She would press it deep onto her bones that were clearly protruding through her thin, wrinkly, loose, almost translucent skin. I concentrated and prayed, hoping the healing energy I was sending through me, from the Source of All, would vitalize her through the ordeal. More than ever I appreciated the training I received from a dear friend and special love, Eleanor, about healing touch and massage, making the most of it during this period. Everything though was in vain.

On Christmas Eve Klaudyna made us a wonderful, traditional, Polish meal. This included potatoes, cabbage, onions, mushrooms and other vegetables. Rebecca, my beautiful 15 year-old daughter was there to help cheer her Grandmother on. When Mom came out of her bedroom to share the meal, she only took one or two bites before returning to her bed. Watching her getting back into bed, I asked myself, "What are we celebrating?" It was clear to me if something didn't shift soon my Mother was going to die. I called my sister, talked with a doctor and Mom agreed to return to the hospital for intravenous fluids and possibly a nasal-gastric or NG feeding tube.

The next morning, I sadly mumbled "Merry Christmas" to myself. We drove Mom to the emergency room where the nurses immediately put an I.V. in her arm for fluids and oxygen in her nose. I stood close by, keeping her warm by adding sheets and blankets over her. Late in the afternoon, now in a regular patients room, three nurses tried to insert a nasal-gastric tube in her nose. It was hard for me to watch two *nurses in training* who were unable to get it in. Under the best of circumstances it's not a pleasant sensation to have this tube put through your nostrils, down to your stomach. It was clearly irritating Mom having them put it in and take it out. I almost yelled, "What are you doing? Get someone who knows how to do it." Finally an experienced nurse did it with no problem. They have to practice on someone, but not on my Mom. She's already discomforted.

Late that same night, way past visiting hours, I persuaded one of the night shift nurses to allow Klaudyna and me into Mom's room. We stayed about an hour, watching Mom twist and turn, moan and groan uncomfortably as she had been doing in her apartment. She opened her eyes once, but didn't acknowledge we were there. We left uncertain if this was going to save her.

The next morning though, she was noticeably more alert and a bit stronger. Standing near her bed, I was a bit mesmerized, watching the life strengthening liquids, slowly drip, drip, drip from the bags into the plastic tubes into her arm and nose. As disdainful as I sometimes am about modern medical technology, it serves a useful purpose. She barely spoke, but with her eyes, and a thin smile on still dried lips, she appreciated us being there, keeping watch.

The tubes stayed in for 48 hours, then on the second night she pulled out the NG tube. It was put back in the next morning. In the afternoon, she pulled it out again. Again it was replaced. That night she pulled the I.V. drip out of her arm and the NG tube out of her nose. They replaced only the feeding tube since the fluids had replenished her, making her strong enough to pull the tube out of her arm.

"Great going mom," I murmured to myself

Every time I went back to see her my plea was to leave in the feeding tube. My plea went unheeded. No explanation about the tubes keeping her alive made a difference. She never admitted she was the one pulling out the tubes. It was obvious she didn't know what she was doing. After putting in the feeding tube four times the nurses became frustrated and finally told her, "You win, Mae, the doctor can deal with you now."

For the next two days I continued trying to persuade her to let them reinsert the feeding tube. She stubbornly refused. "I can't stand it Robert. I can't breath. I don't want it." The hospital kitchen continued to bring her trays of food for each meal, but she only managed a few sips of soup or a few spoons of oatmeal. This was now past her fourth week without a meal. Again, I told myself, her life couldn't go on much longer.

The fourth morning she woke and her voice was

almost gone. No one diagnosed the cause, but the nurses suggested, and I figured as much, that she irritated her throat when she roughly pulled out the NG tube. Her lungs also, overnight, became very congested, with deep, gurgling coughs. A nurse told me that one of the times when the feeding tube was reinserted it went into her lungs and not her stomach. It was all awkward: My mother who trusts the medical world as if they wore divine halos, were not only unable to help her, but in fact, were contributing to her discomfort and dilemma.

She was at a very critical juncture. I called her doctor who suggested a gastric feeding tube, a g-tube that goes directly into the stomach through the abdominal wall. He said, "Your mother is demented and I don't know what else to do for her."

It was like an insult to her; since she wasn't demented, although now, very confused. He was a bit pushy. I didn't like listening to him. He sounded like a used car salesman trying to convince me of something we didn't want to buy. In my mind I said, "No thank you Dr. Frankenstein." If she had a feeding tube it might mean she would have to go to a nursing home. I had seen some patients pull the g-tube out of their stomach. We already had enough of that.

Later in the day in a conversation with my sister we talked about the feeding tube and agreed to let our Mom decide. She had decided against that when she was in her apartment. She didn't change her mind when we talked that evening. She said, "I want to wait for a miracle." A miracle. My mother wanted a miracle. I wanted one too.

"Let's see what we can do." I am a person who takes charge and doesn't mind challenges. In the nursing home where I work as the social worker frequently my efforts went beyond the scope of my job description, but this wasn't just any challenge, it was my Mother. I had to do something.

Early on New Years Eve sitting on my Mom's hospital bed, looking at her wasting away body it became very clear to me she couldn't stay in the hospital any longer. She would have to come to my house. What difference it would make from when she was in her own apartment, no one could say. But if she was going to die, I know she wouldn't want it to be in a hospital. I had to tell her straight up, "Mom, you are getting close to dying and the option of coming to my house is what you have to do. I'll be there after work." She nodded. "Mom, my kids can help, Klaudyna can help for a while. She's returning to Poland next week then I'll find someone else to help out." She was so weak, with barely an audible voice, rasping a few times, "Robert, I'm so tired. I'm ready for a pill to put me to sleep."

"I know how you're feeling mom, but let's give this a try. We all love you and want to help."

Our talk on New Years Eve was sacred and a bit surreal. Maybe all my talks with nursing home residents before they left this plane were practice for talking to my Mom. Asking myself, "What kind of conversation is this? Where does it come from? Why is it happening?" It was all so deep within me, being certain, this was the only alternative. It touched me as deeply as any moment in my life. I wondered if this was one of those moments when God-Allah, the Creator of All Life comes through, as me, for me to be the best I could be.

She was partially conscious, but knew she was leaving the hospital and felt a relief. "They have no time for me Robert. They are in and then out to take care of someone else." It didn't matter how many times we explained hospital procedures, other patients to attend to—she wanted more attention. Join the club Mom. She felt assured she would get what she needed at my house along with the love she needed.

She asked for a miracle: I was reaching for one.

On January 2nd we brought my Mother to my home in a wheelchair. She was too weak to walk. It was a Friday night, and although I didn't usually observe the Jewish Sabbath, this was no usual Friday night. My Mother is indifferent to this also, but instead of waiting in bed, where she spent most of the past month, she sat in the wheelchair by the kitchen. She wanted to be part of what was going on as we prepared the special meal. It was a surprise and a delight to see her energy and interest.

I said a prayer over the challah, the ritual braided bread for Sabbath; said a prayer over the Sabbath wine, and made a special prayer for my Mother when lighting the Sabbath candles: "May my Mother be engulfed and strengthened by the holiness from the light of the Sabbath candles. May the holy female energy, Shekinah, the Goddess of Sabbath, help my Mother on her way."

Although being deeply a spiritual person, my prayers were never for her to live; only asking Life to do what was best for her. There is a deep abiding faith in me everything happens for a reason.

Mom was unable to eat that first night, but she did take a morsel of the challah and sipped the wine. She sat through part of the meal with Klaudyna, Rebecca and myself then went back into bed.

She never used the wheelchair again, insisting on walking alone, holding on to furniture and the wall. She was ready to reestablish herself as a whole person again. It wasn't safe walking alone, but when she insists no one wins an argument with her, even if she is wrong. We walked with her the first two days, but she persisted. What was there to say, but, "Okay Mom, you're on your own?" From that day on she began to very slowly eat, gradually regaining her strength. The Hospice staff came to see her along with their doctor who said, "Mae, I probably won't see you again, not because you're going to die, but you are going to revive." She will survive this.

Odd, but even though she was so close to death, once she was in my house I knew she was going to make it.

Her friends called it a miracle. It was beyond me what to call it except that she responded to love, home cooking and special attention from her family in a home atmosphere. Was it the light and energy from Chanukah, Christmas, and Sabbath candles, Shekinah? Who knows maybe that and maybe more. It wasn't her time. She didn't want to die. She had the will to live. My Mom lived with me for four months. During the last month, when she was back to her old self I had had enough. She was too strong willed, determined to have things only her way. We began our old pattern of arguing over everything. I had to check myself a number of times, becoming angry and yelling at this frail, old, woman. My fault, her tenacity, whatever it was we had come to a conclusion. When Klaudyna left for Poland after the first week, a friend recommended a woman to be with mom during the day, but working full time and caring for her after work was too much for me.

I moved her back into her apartment. She was welcomed back by all her friends. They called her the "Miracle Lady."

She lived at the Atrium for four more years, enjoying her friends, laughing, dancing, playing poker with a group she organized and getting loving attention from her friend John. Having been so close to death she appreciated this bonus tagged on to her life. It was a bonus for me also, as I regularly took her out for meals, movies, or to the mall so she could window shop and, browse as a consummate "Mall Queen," of our culture. It was far from my favorite way to spend time, but it made me feel good giving her what made her feel good.

After those four bonus years, my mother again needed to come live with me one more time when she was no longer able to take care of herself. This time it was for seven months, the last months of her life.

# Three Vignettes About Dad

The following are three vignettes from a running narrative I kept about taking care of my father who had mid to late stages of Alzheimer's disease.

## Dad Goes for a Swim

It was a beautiful sunny North Florida day when I took my Dad for a visit to friends who lived near a small lake out in the country. After a few of us sat and talked for a while, we decided to walk down to the lake, which was about 100 feet from the house. I asked Dad if he wanted to swim with us, but he declined saying, "No, I'll sit here on the porch." I pointed down to the water to show him where we would be, telling him he could see us from the porch. I asked him to stay on the porch and we'd be up in a short while. As usual, he was agreeable.

After we were in the lake for fifteen minutes, I looked up to the house and saw Dad trucking down to the lake. It wasn't a long walk, but on the uneven grass covered ground, sloping to the lake, he was moving slow and carefully. I came out of the water to meet and talk with him about what he wanted to do. In a proud, somewhat vain way, with his famous smile, he said, as if he did this all the time, "I'm going swimming, what do you think?" Yeah, what did I think? What I thought was: This is love being out here with my father. There was total gratitude in me for the opportunity to care for my Father and now taking him for a swim.

Not wanting to lose the moment, I quickly decided not to get his bathing suit from the car. I began to help him off with his tennis shoes and socks and asked him if he wanted to take off his shorts and swim in is underpants. As expected he said, "No, I don't do that, I'll go in my shorts."

He approached the water tentatively, with me holding his hand. He stopped at the water's edge and began to take off his shorts, saw his underpants and pulled up on the shorts. He again said, "I don't want to swim in my underpants."

In the water, ankle deep, I was surprised how very, slow-motion-like he was walking into the shallow water. When the water was only up to his calf, he had a hard time walking forward. He began to lean backward. Soon, with me still holding his hand, his balance and mine were lost as we slowly, laughing, went down into sitting positions. I asked him if he wanted to remain sitting in the water. "No, I'm here to go swimming." I helped him back up and we continued walking out further where the others were swimming and talking. Although he continued to appear a bit uncertain about what he was doing, he had this amazing, broad grin on his face during this whole time. I loved seeing this grin. It reminded me of when he was younger and with mind.

My Dad worked for twenty-seven years in Rheingold Brewery in Orange, New Jersey. Maybe if he drank more beer his mind might still be there. He'd get a case of beer for Christmas—the bonus. It sat in the basement for months, with him occasionally bringing up a couple cans. Then they would sit in the refrigerator for days before he'd drink a can; usually on the weekend, sitting in the back yard or watching a baseball game on T.V.

I asked him, just checking, knowing the answer: "Dad do you remember how to swim?"

"Sure, how can one forget to swim?" he said with total confidence.

Actually he had been an excellent swimmer. Almost every morning for 20 years he would swim in the pool of the condo for 20 minutes. As a young man he used to swim in the ocean, long distances, paralleling the beach. As the dementia took hold he went out for his daily swim less and less, and now hadn't been swimming for at least two years.

Even though he was expressing confidence in his intention, I had to keep encouraging him to move his feet forward. It was the same on dry ground. On sidewalks or wherever, he would stop walking for no reason except his brain cells weren't sending the walking messages to his feet to move them. Sometimes he would slowly crumple to the ground or floor when those messages didn't tell him to stand. "Dad, keep walking," I would tell him. "You're going down to the floor." "No, I'm not," he'd say to me, I'm walking," as one knee was already on the ground.

But today, in an accustomed place, with the friendly, familiar water, he was slowly moving along, almost other species like, or a primordial self, being called, returning to a previous incarnation. At some point my friend, Nancy, walked over to join us, taking dad's other hand. Now with the added support he moved further out with more certainty. After taking fifteen minutes for a twenty-foot walk, we were to where the water was still only just above his waist, but that was his sign, as he began pulling on our hands to let go. He immediately submerged his body, coming up blowing water out of his mouth, giving off a sound, like an ancient sea animal. Then he began his simple crawl stroke: his right arm lifting out of the water, his left pulling underneath, his face going in on each stroke, slowly coming out each time his arm surfaced, blowing out, taking a breath, his legs slowly moving underneath, never breaking the surface with even a ripple. He was moving along as rhythmically as in the past. I walked along side of him until we were out above my neck when I asked him to turn around. I wasn't sure if he heard me, with his head going in and out, but he turned, continuing his stroke towards shore. Nancy remained on one side, me on the other. Once he had his familiar rhythm, he didn't stop going in circles for 20 minutes, except to occasionally stand, look around, and then continue his stroke. Two or three times he would put his face in the water, bubbling underneath. Then he came up to take some air, doing some kind of rest for himself. After he had his fill, his feet on the mushy sand, he started walking towards the shore. I remained by his side the whole time as Nancy was back with the others.

He showed no exhaustion from his swim, but I wasn't sure if he could walk back up the sloping field to the house. I asked him, "Dad, do you want me to get the car?" "No, I can walk," which he did without shoes. I held his hand part of the way, but he pulled it away not wanting or needing the support. Not feeling any exertion, he walked to the house.

Later, when our friends were back at the house they complimented his swimming. He brushed it off as "Not much of a swim," having a sense of who he used to be.

When we were home, as usual, I asked him, "Dad, how'd you like the swim?" He had no recollection at all. I knew that, so why did I ask? Was it only for me to see if something stuck of the wonderful experience? Did a part of me want us to remember and share the memory together? Maybe this time it would be different and he would remember. Did it matter? Not to him, with Buddha mind, aware only of the moment; with almost no awareness of self, big or small young or old. Maybe though, it was enough being the ancient at-peace-sea-animal who experienced this brief stint as a caring, non-violent, human being. I am thankful he passed that legacy of being on to me and me in turn to my children.

## Who's Who?

The morning: Time to change Dad's diaper; help get him dressed and give him breakfast. Then he'll be ready for his day at the Alzheimer's program.

I walked into Dad's bedroom where he was contentedly looking out the window at the beautiful, purple, blooming, azaleas.

"Hi Pop," he says with his big smile, "look at my flowers."

This time I ignore him calling me "Pop."

"They're pretty Dad and they're all for you. Some are even peeking under the window so you can touch them. You're lucky to have them so close to touch. I need to change your diaper. It's probably wet."

"What diaper?"

"The one you're wearing. You had it on all night. I'm sure it's wet."

"What'aya talking about? I don't have a diaper."

"Yeah you do Dad, you forget. I keep reminding you about things but you forget as soon as I tell you."

"I do?"

"Yeah, you do. So here, I'll show you your diaper."

I took off his pajamas and showed him the diaper. He looked at them but said nothing. I went to the bathroom and brought back a washcloth and towel. I wiped and dried him then put on some Argo Cornstarch.

He looked at the yellow box, with the word "Argo" on it and smiled. "Argo, Argo fuck your self," then laughed. I laugh with him. It was almost like a vaudeville routine. Something about my Dad remembering the Argo line each morning made me feel good. It reminds me of his regular sense of humor when he had memory.

After he's changed and dressed, I ask him, "Okay Dad, ready for some breakfast?"

He smiled. "I'm always ready to eat. What you got, Pop?"

"Dad, I'm your son, not your pop."

He looks at me as if I was lying. "Dad, I remind you

of this every day. You and Mom, Mae, your wife, had me 55 years ago. Believe me, you're my father. I'm your son."

"Your 55? How could you be 55? I'm about 56."

"Dad, you're 80. You're a grandpa. My kids live here with us. They help take care of you."

"They do?"

Sometimes I get tired of the routine. Was it for me? Was there something in me that needed to keep trying to get him to know what was going on? He didn't care, why should I? He was content. *Almost* total and complete contentment. If everyone were as content as he was in his life, we'd have a much saner world. Not much would get done, but maybe too much gets done anyway. There is something amazing about him. He didn't expect too much out of life, didn't put out a whole lot to make things happen; he didn't even say too much. Something in him though, always seemed content with the way things were, are. Why do I have to try and get him now to understand what's going on? He smiles, he laughs, and he enjoys his days, just like when he had a thinking mind. What's the difference if he doesn't have a memory?

"Come on Dad, stand up. I'll help you out of bed and get you dressed. You can come into the dinning area and I'll get you breakfast. What do you want?"

"Yeah, just give me anything. What you got?"

"I'll squeeze a couple of oranges, then fix some Cheerios with raisins, bananas and soy milk."

"Sounds good. I'll have that."

After I set it all on the table for him and he was sitting eating, I went outside to hang the sheets and his bedclothes on the line. Hanging stuff in the Florida sun is so much better than using the dryer. One day I counted how long the clotheslines were—three of them, each 50 feet long. Am I a mad man, 150 feet of clothes hanging on clotheslines on principle? My kids won't do it. Typically, they told me to take it to the laundromat. I persist and do it myself.

When I came back into the kitchen he was all done eating what I had put out for him.

"Here Dad let me take your bowl and cup."

"What for?"

"You finished eating breakfast. I'll wash the bowl and cup."

"I didn't have anything to eat yet. I'm still waiting."

A half smile came to my face. "Dad, here's your bowl and cup from your cereal and juice."

"No, it isn't. I didn't have anything, yet."

"Yeah, Dad, you did. Believe me. I made it for you. Then put it on the table. You ate it while I was outside hanging clothes on the line. Good man, Dad. It's a blessing your a good eater." Again, trying to convince him of a reality he can't remember.

Then, in an angry, loud voice, "Don't tell me I ate breakfast. I didn't have anything." Not a 100% content: 90% Buddha mind, 10% dementia, maybe manifesting energy from someplace in him that has been held back. Arguing is useless; I'll get something. "You want some toast and tea?"

"Yeah, give me some toast and tea. If that's all you'll give me, then give me that. They don't feed me here."

"We feed you good Dad; the best food around. Some of it's right from the backyard garden. You know, I give you peas to eat from the garden, and the greens for the salad. You like them." I can't stop myself trying to help him remember.

"I do. You grow food here?"

"Yes, we do Dad. You've been out back a lot and have been in the garden. You like it."

"I do?"

"Yes, you do. Here's the tea and toast. Enjoy it."

"What are you going to do pop?"

"I have to get ready for work Dad."

"You work?"

"Yeah, I work at a hospital as a social worker. I have to go soon. Traci, the young black lady will be coming to stay with you soon. You know Traci. She comes every morning when I go to work. She helps take care of you."

"What kind of help do I need?"

"Anything Dad. She'll help you with food, or change your clothes, or take you out for a ride. Actually today you go to the Alzheimer's program. They'll pick you up."

"The bus."

"Yeah, the bus." A breakthrough, not a big one, but he remembers the bus. "You remember taking the bus?"

"Sure I know about the bus. Why shouldn't I remember the bus?"

"You know where it takes you?"

"No, where does it take me?"

I'm tired of it. I have to get to work. My patience gets thin sometimes. "It doesn't matter Dad. I have to get ready. Traci just pulled into the driveway and will be here with you until the bus comes. I'll see you later. One last thing: The bus takes you to the Alzheimer's program. I love you Dad. See you later."

As I'm going out the door, I turn my head to look at him, and tell him again, "I love you Dad. He smiles: "I love you too pop."

## My Dad Still Can Dance

One summer evening I decided to take my Dad to a dance with live music sponsored by the Arts and Medicine program in the hospital where I worked.

"Dad," I said, "we're going to hear some music tonight. Maybe there'll be some dancing."

"Music," he responded, "who wants to hear music?"

My Dad who had Alzheimer's disease lived with my three adolescent children and myself.

"You like to listen to music, Dad. We heard some last week at the Plaza." I knew he didn't remember the incident, but he always liked to watch and listen to live music.

"I like music?"

"Yeah, you do," I said with a hopeful smile. "There'll be dancing too."

"Who's going to dance?"

"Maybe you will. You used to like to dance with Mom."

"Oh yeah, dancing with Mom. Whose mom? Where'd she go?"

"My Mom, your wife, Mae. You danced with her at the condo, when they had entertainment at night."

"I did?"

"Yeah, you did." I didn't want to get into a whole

discussion, but I was trying to create some interest and again to stimulate his memory, even though I knew it was usually futile. "Come on, we'll have a good time. I'll help you get your shoes on."

"What do I need help with my shoes for? I can get my shoes on." Sometimes he managed them well, and sometimes he had socks over shoes, shoes over slippers, or any mix and match that came together for him.

I sat across from his bed as he took off his slippers. He held each shoe in his hands looking at them before he decided which foot it went on. Then he put his slippers over the toes of his shoes. He looked at them a few seconds, looked at me, and we laughed together. "That doesn't look right," he said. He took off the slippers and started to take off the shoes.

"No Dad, leave your shoes on, we're going to hear some music and maybe dance." He left them on; tied the shoes, and said, "Okay Pop, where're we going?"

Ever since my Father had been living with us, he began to call me "Pop." It bothered me some since I was taking care of him and would have liked for him to know who I was. Another side of me though knew this was for him. Again, I kindly reminded him, "Dad, you're the pop, I'm the son." It really didn't matter, but still I had to say it. It's impossible to know the workings of a mind lost in dementia. Since we were living with my three children and I was the man with the gray beard—I must be "Pop."

"We're going to hear some music Dad."

"Well, I'm waiting for you Pop," he said, "What's taking you so long?"

My Dad lived with us for two years. During that

period, I was working full time in a hospital as a medical social worker. Compared to some, my Dad's dementia was relatively easy to work with and it had not destroyed his general good nature. He had his bouts of confusion, and sometimes would get angry yelling at my children when he didn't recognize who they were. On two occasions he walked out of the house alone: One time in his underpants carrying a tennis racket in one hand and his truss in the other. He got lost, but thankfully we found him in a near-by wooded area leaning against a tree.

Often at night, I had to check on him two and three times when I heard him talking to himself in his bedroom. I would get up and change his sheets and bedclothes. Some nights he would climb over the bedrail of the hospital bed and I'd find him on the floor. I'd help him into a chair, change his wet sheets and pajamas, help him back into bed, and hope I didn't have to get up again.

I was fortunate that my children were able to give some help, taking him for walks or staying with him at home if I was out for a bit. There was a part time caregiver when I was at work, but really it was all on me—a full time job, three children, plus my Father. I loved my Dad very much, especially because he had an exceptionally gentle spirit. Yet, some days while driving to work after a difficult night, I'd ask myself, "How much am I supposed to handle?" I didn't like to admit it, but I had my limits. With a bit of guilt, I wondered, "When will this end?"

When we arrived at the gym where the dance was being held, we sat on chairs near the dance floor. When a few friends of mine came over to say hello, Dad responded with a great big friendly smile. As soon as the music started, he began to tap his feet and sway his body. It made me feel good to see him, at 80 years old, so taken in by the music. Soon after the band began, Lu Ann, a young nurse I knew from the hospital where we worked, came over to talk with us a couple of times. I appreciated her being especially friendly and warm towards my Father. She finally asked me if he could dance. "Sure, he would like that." I moved away from him a bit and whispered to her, "He falls sometimes and has dementia, but he loves to dance."

My Dad actually fell a lot. I'd estimated he must have fallen between fifty and a hundred times while he lived with us. Miraculously, and maybe being strong boned, he never injured himself. We considered getting him a walker, but because his balance was off and with his dementia, I knew he wouldn't have been able manage one.

When Lu Ann held out her hand and asked him to dance, Dad's hand reflexively went out and together they walked, holding hands onto the dance floor. There was a small turnout of about 20 people and no one was on the dance floor yet, so it was all theirs. She started off carefully, as she gauged his ability. Then she began to move a bit more as he was getting the feel for the rhythm. His face took on a broad glowing smile. His body moved a bit stiffly, but as he moved about I could see his obvious remembrance of past years. I was surprised at how well he followed her steps. They danced two numbers then she walked him back to his chair—the glowing smile still radiating on his face.

Lu Ann came back for him and again led him onto the dance floor. This time the music was a bit faster so she held him closer to give him more support. She kept him going for almost half an hour. My Dad loved every minute. At some point though, I could see him getting a bit tired from his enjoyable workout.

It was the first time we had done anything like this. Usually I took Dad out for walks, to restaurants, to visit my friends or to the downtown Plaza to see live music. Tonight, though, was definitely a hit all around. Dad and I both hugged LuAnn and thanked her for the dances. When we came home, I helped Dad put on his pajamas and left him sitting on his bed for a few minutes. When I came back he was lying in bed with three hats on.

"Dad, why do you have three hats on?"

"I have three hats?"

"Yeah, you do."

He took one off, looked at it and put it back on his head. "There that's better."

I was used to him sometimes going to bed with more than one hat and realized early on, in the midst of everything, wearing three hats really didn't matter. Out of curiosity, I had to ask him, "Dad, did you like dancing with that pretty young woman?"

He looked at me with a questioning expression. "What dance? What woman?"

That was it—another good time with my Father. Like a good Buddha, he enjoyed the present moment and went on to the next, three hats and no worries.

Not too long after I took my Dad to the dance, there was a call from *Alz Place,* the Alzheimer's Day Program he attended. They told me he just sort of crumbled to the floor. His hip broke apart. He was taken to the hospital where it was repaired with a plate and bolts.

It took some soul searching, but I had the answer to the question I had posed to myself: "How much can I do?" I knew my Dad wasn't going to walk with his hip damaged. I wouldn't be able to manage him at home. To move him in and out of bed, dress him, change his wet diapers—all that it took would be beyond my capabilities. As much as I didn't want to, I had him admitted to a nursing home near where I worked. My Dad lived there contentedly for two more years. And there, finally, when I came to see him, he would proudly say with a smile, "Oh, there's my son."

# Changing Mary's Diapers

Mary was only 73, but now so frail and weak she could barely stand on her own. She even needed help to get to the potty near her bed. When I came into her room to see how she was doing she was lying in bed with her smile that was so familiar to me. My ex-wife, Linda, and I, helped care for Mary in our home for more than 10 years. We both felt much affection for her. Now, in those moments, we both had a deep appreciation to have the opportunity to help her as she was weakening.

But changing her diaper? Linda was out for the day—changing Mary's diapers were part of her job—I was alone with Mary. How was I going to manage?

Standing for a few breaths I savored the moments looking at Mary's angelic face that had brought so much joy to our family. Mary had been sick off and on for the past two years her body becoming weaker and weaker. One function after another was shutting down. Linda and I both wondered if she was going to die soon. Now, here alone in the house, her diaper was probably wet.

A brief thought flashed into my mind of our three

children whose diapers I had frequently changed, but Mary, a woman, an elder: There was a slightly uncomfortable feeling in me as I mentally prepared myself to help her.

"Mary, is your diaper wet?"

She smiled and said, "How nice."

Her ever present smile and her favorite expression, "How nice," had both been with us since she came to live in our personal care home for "only" a few weeks after having a stroke. She needed to be close to a hospital where she was to receive speech therapy. Because of the way the stroke affected her brain, she wasn't able to get her speech pattern even close to normal. Fortunately right from the beginning she understood everything and communicated as best as she could.

As we moved from West Virginia to Pennsylvania to Florida Mary never stopped living with us. Now here we were, with Mary having become such a close family member we considered her a surrogate grandmother.

I tried quietly again, "Mary, do you need your diaper changed? Are you uncomfortable?"

She smiled again, nodding her head, but with her weakness it was unclear which way she was nodding, up, down or sideways. Be patient, I reminded myself.

"You haven't been to the potty for a few hours. Why don't we take a look and see if you need to be changed?

I walked tentatively to her bed as she began to pull back her sheets.

"Here, let me give you a hand with your sheet." Her nightgown was up to her thighs and I could see how thin she had become in the past year. Never heavy, she was

30

now mostly sagging flesh with bones jutting out. She smiled and nodded thanks.

"Mary, I never changed an adult's diaper, but you saw me do it with the kids many times so we should make out okay. You don't mind me helping you, do you? Linda is away for the day and I'm the only one home." She smiled and tried to sit up.

"Wait Mary, let me help you," as I put my arm around her back and helped her into a sitting position. Then eased her legs around off the bed. Mary was short; her feet almost touched the floor. "Do you want to go to the potty?" She didn't answer, but put her hands on the bed as she tried to push herself onto her feet. "Slow down, I'll get you over to the potty."

I helped her across the few steps to the potty then gave support and positioned her in front of the potty chair. "Can you stand okay while we take off the diapers? Hold onto my shoulders and I'll get these off."

I felt under the plastic to the wet diaper. "Yes, they are wet, you must have been uncomfortable. Maybe we should hook up a bell like we used to have so you can ring us if you're wet or need something. What do you think?"

It wasn't clear if Mary thought of much anymore, but it was familiar talking with her, even if the conversation had become more one-sided as she weakened. And the bell, we stopped hanging it on the bedpost when she was no longer alert enough to use it.

After managing to get the plastics off, the Attends slid down by her ankles. "You're going to have to hold on and lift a leg again so we can get this wet diaper off." She knew the routine staying steady putting one hand on my shoulder as she lifted one leg and then the other. This stage was over.

With that done, the next step was easing her down onto the potty chair. "Mary, I'll wait right outside by the door so you have privacy." A smile came onto my face of the words just spoken to Mary. They repeated themselves in my mind. Here I was helping her out of a diaper; as intimate as a human interaction can be, but yet the customary privacy offered as she sat on the plastic potty chair. I wondered, for a moment, about the loss of self-esteem many must feel when they need this kind of assistance. It didn't seem to apply to Mary who we helped for so many years.

It crossed my mind if there was a concern about anything happening to her being left alone on the potty?

After a few minutes there was the tinkle in the bucket. I poked my head in the room. "Are you done Mary?" She smiled as she was trying to stand. "No wait, let me give you paper to wipe yourself." Handing her the paper with the realization I should have done that before leaving the room. "Mary, "I'll go out of the room while you clean yourself and then give you a washcloth to wipe your hands."

After putting warm water on the washcloth I came back into the room, and found her half on her bed and half on the floor. She was just hanging on. "Mary, what are you trying to do? Wait, let me give you a hand to help get you onto the bed." She smiled and nodded as I helped her into a sitting position on the side of the bed. "Here's a washcloth." She took the washcloth and diligently cleaned each finger, her palms, then and the backs of her hands.

She handed me the washcloth and started to turn herself around into a lying position.

"Wait, Mary, let's get a dry diaper on you." An odd thought crossed my mind whether it was easier to get it on if she was lying down or sitting. How did Linda do it? I realized I didn't pay much attention when it was being done. With young babies they were always lying down, so, "Mary lie down, we'll get them on you." With my arms around her, I lifted her legs onto the bed and she was in position. One of the diapers was out of the box. Looking at it and laughing quietly to myself, not having any idea, which way it went on.

My thoughts rambled a bit: Maybe paying attention when Linda changed Mary would have been wise. Maybe there should be a nurse; maybe I should be a nurse. Why am I changing the diaper of a 73-year-old woman? Come on get serious, she's been a friend, a surrogate grandmother to our kids, almost like an angel in our home. She has been a gift; like a resident angel. The words to a Shaker song, "Tis a Gift to be Simple," popped into memory. So if Mary is an angel, what am I doing helping change her diaper? Am I worthy to do this for an angel? No time to ponder philosophical meanderings, she's on the bed, nightgown up to her knees waiting for help.

"Okay, Mary, it goes this way or no, maybe this way," as I held the diaper in front of me turning it around a few times. It reminded me of the first time I put disposables on the kids. Did it matter which way? Mary reached for the diaper and turned it into position trying to raise her self a bit. "Here let me lift you and get this under you." She made it easy. Soon the diaper was on, then the plastic over it and we were done.

"We did it, Mary. Are you comfortable?" She smiled. "Do you need anything else? Are you hungry? I'll get you some soup I made earlier today. She smiled again and said, "How nice," as I left her room.

It wasn't too long after my special afternoon with Mary when she had another stroke resulting in a brain hemorrhage. The doctors told us any invasive surgery was chancy. From what we discussed with Mary previously, we knew it would have been her decision to not have anything done. We asked the staff on the Intensive Care Unit to let us know when her time was close. Within two days we received a call from the hospital telling us it was that time. Linda and I picked up our two sons, Jacob nine and Gabriel seven from grammar school, and with our four-year-old daughter, Rebecca, we all were by her beside when she took her last breath. We were so grateful the staff brought Mary from the ICU into a private room and allowed our children to be there with us.

Three years earlier we thought Mary was going to die. To comfort her, we allowed our sons to lovingly crawl underneath and around her bed as we let Rebecca, who was only one to lie with Mary on her bed. We told them, "Be quiet and gentle to Mary, she is very sick. Their presence, so close to her, helped put a familiar smile back on her face. Unknowingly, they were doing a children's healing dance for Mary and now, how sweet, being with her, as she left this plane.

# Amazing Grace

After helping take care of Mac for the past year, I, along with his daughters and the other caregivers expected him to leave this life soon. This particular evening I came to Mac's house at 6:00 p.m. as a favor to relieve Lynn, another caregiver, for three hours. She was going to a Buddhist meditation class. Joan, one of Mac's daughters, and her husband Bill were going out to get something to eat. They would all be back later in the evening.

When I first came to the house that evening, Joan took my hand and asked me, "Please, Bob come say good night to my father." She actually pulled on me a bit. It felt like a pull of appreciation. During the past year I was the main caregiver for Mac and had become close to him as well as to his daughters. She also may have felt some angst about what we knew was imminent. At this critical time she wanted me to come in to see her father. I had been hired through an agency to help Mac with his day-to-day activities. During the past year my energies were also for his daughters, as a friend and informal counselor. As I walked with her to Mac's bedroom, Joan gave me a brief update on her father. She told me she and Lynn had just changed her dad's sheets. They also gave him a sip of water. Mac appeared to be asleep, but I wished him a good night anyway and we left his room.

After they all left, I sat in the living room reading for a few minutes, but soon, felt a strong impulse, like a pull on me to be in the bedroom with Mac. He was in his last days. At 89 years old, he was now down to half his 180 pounds.

I sat down on a chair next to Mac's bed and looked at his emaciated face as his mouth hung limply open. There was a tired worn down expression on his face. For the past few weeks his face appeared this way when he slept. It only took me a few breaths to realize he had already left his body. Nevertheless I kept checking to make sure it wasn't a mistake since there was a slight movement of the sheet over his body and fifteen minutes ago Joan told me they just gave him some water. "What's going on here? Is he or isn't he?" He looked like he had stopped breathing. It was a bit bewildering, watching the slight movement on the sheet. Something in me felt weird, not knowing. Finally, my left hand gently pulled the sheet off him as I rested my right hand on his chest; with the sheet off, there it was—a slight pulse just below the zyphoid, the center point at the tip of his rib cage.

Being finally convinced he had left or actually was in the process of leaving his body, a deep part of my inner self felt it was my place to help him with his transition. It crossed my mind to call Mac's daughters, but something in me felt being here alone with Mac was for a reason. Joan would be back soon, then she could call her sister Lou and they would call the funeral home.

I'm comfortable with the process of death, having been with over 15 people before, during, or just after they took their last breath. Over the years, I've come to understand it's a gift brought to me in this life: A calling, even though I never heard an audible voice.

My belief is we can be sensitive to know when we hear a call from the Divine. This call comes from a higher place inside of us—our connection to the Creator. It is different than our usual ego-thinking mind. To be present to this call, trusting my higher self has been a guideline for my path in life. This moment felt that way.

Sitting with Mac in those special moments, my consciousness, maybe more, my soul, deep within, felt moved to try and help clear away the disturbing influences that might prevent him from having a peaceful transition. Mac was a tormented man. This was especially true in the last two weeks when he screamed and yelled in his sleep, as he called out for help. This had gone on, to a lesser degree, for two months, but more recently, his screaming was more intense. At night hearing him scream, I would jump up from the couch or out of bed and rush into his bedroom to see what was happening to him. Usually he was asleep, sometimes not. "What's going on Mac? Were you dreaming?" He never told me or anyone else anything? Either he had no recollection of his disturbing sleep experience, or he was unable to share it.

It was disconcerting to hear the anguished call for help from a person I had come to know well and loved. I cared deeply about what he was going through. He would soon be leaving this life yet here he was screaming out, yelling, "Help me, help me." As I write I can still hear his anguished voice. His two daughters, as well as the other caregivers, had all experienced these episodes.

There was a deep feeling of empathy in me for his inner conflict. Sitting close to his inert body, there was misty-eyed questioning in me about how long he had suffered. Could it be for more than 60 years? Mac was a Marine on one of the ships in Pearl Harbor the morning of the Japanese bombings? Were there imprints in his memory from when he helped pull fellow Marines—boys really—out of the water—some dead, some alive? I didn't want to, but I could almost hear them calling, "Help me, help me." It was impossible to imagine what that was like. His daughters had no clue since he never shared that pain, only a bit of the experience.

There's a Buddhist practice for people who are leaving this plain, especially for those who are suffering. It is called tonglen. I did this practice for Mac off and on for many months. In the mornings of my three times a week 24 hour shifts, this practice was added to my regular meditation. I did it while Mac was asleep in his bedroom on the other side of a thin wall. It was my attempt to try to help dissolve some of the dark mist that surrounded him, disturbing his peace. In the end—it's sad to say or think—but it felt as if demons of one sort or another— those imprints and images from the war—were pursuing Mac. Buddhism calls them demons; psychology calls them impressions in our unconscious. The least I could do was try to dissolve some of the misty darkness and transpose it into light, and send it back to him.

Now, here I was, with his life force actually leaving his body. There was a sense of shocked awe in me, with an acute awareness of the synchronicity, the timing, of my being asked to relieve Lynn for three hours while she went to her meditation class. Reaching out in prayer, in my deepest sense of consciousness and wonder, sitting with Mac, trying to grasp how things happen in life. How *was* this moment happening? At times, when Mac was in his declining stages and my shift was over, while getting into my car, it would cross my mind whether he would depart from this plain when I was away. Something in my nature wanted to be there. And now, these moments: For him and me? This wasn't a planned event. At least none Mac or I planned. Or was it planned? If my deepest self, the soul part of my being, wanted it to be this way, could I have willed it? Either way, it furthered my belief in the workings of the universe: nothing occurs at random.

This is all deep in my essence. Going over my notes 15 months after Mac's passing, there is a psychophysical sensation pulsing through me of that time with him.

Sitting with Mac, my thoughts briefly were with Lynn appreciating her being at a Buddhist meditation class probably doing some concentrations for Mac. It was all so appropriate. I gently rubbed Mac's crown charka on the top of his head. This is a Hindu practice to help spiritual energies leave the body from that point. Having studied different spiritual practices about what to do at this stage I was thankful for my path in life bringing me these teachings. In those moments—only one desire—that Mac should be at peace.

I sat with Mac for over ninety minutes until Lynn returned, then Mac's daughter and son-in-law who called Joan's sister, then the funeral home.

The day after Mac passed there was a very odd transition for me, being hired to be with another partially disabled man, Leo. It was my first 24-hour shift with him. In wanting to help this man, on my first day, being totally engrossed, somehow Mac was totally forgotten. Sometime later, I questioned my self: "How did I forget such a strong, emotional incident?" My first thought was that it happened because of my need to be present for this new man, Leo. In deeper reflection though, it seemed like more—that those moments with Mac happened in a period of timelessness.

Now here I was standing in Leo's kitchen reflecting on the bells I had just attached to Leo's walker right next to his bed. This was done so he could shake the bells to wake me during the night if he needed help with the hand-held urinal. Standing in the kitchen, I heard bells making noise. Mac had Christmas bells on his walker for the same reason. I knew the bells ringing didn't sound like the ones just put on Leo's walker. Nevertheless I quickly went to Leo's bedroom. He was in deep sleep. Back in the kitchen and again there were the bells. "What's going on here?" But I knew-believed-felt, Mac was letting me know he still needed help. With no doubt in my mind, but slightly mystified, I went into my sleeping room and put on my prayer shawl and meditation cap, the same ones' worn for a year during my meditations in what was Mac's office. I sat and prayed, concentrated and meditated to be with Mac in my highest means of consciousness. I needed to be where he was, to do what could be done to ease his pain. This sacred dance was a part of my being, having some comprehension of what is right from studies in Sufi mysticism and other esoteric teachings.

Being able to be with Mac there was a trust in the higher parts of who I am. Many of us know from first hand experiences, of the energetic connections and communications—non-local consciousness—that exists between people on various levels and from various distances on this material plain. And there is more: Connections, communications, do happen between different planes of existence. There is more to this life than what goes on through our senses—this is known to me with certainty.

In the next few days there were more connections with Mac. I sent him similar prayers of strength and guidance. And then, those particular connections with him began to diminish. Yet, 15 months later there are still felt emotions from the experience with Mac.

Here, now, sitting, writing, my attempt to get words down so others may understand. Yes, this is a belief of mine: My work-into-stories of the sick, the poor, the dying, the homeless, is for others to get a glimpse of another other who is a part of this one life.

Odd, how I came to do a job to help Mac, and it turned out to be not a job, but the *highest work* of life. I was receiving a gift from the Divine to as present as possible.

Two days prior to his last breath, on my regular 24-hour shift, I spent some time sitting with Mac while he was in bed. Something in me thought it might be important to remind him I was a minister, in case he wanted to share something. As he lay in his bed, his hands automatically went into a prayer position. A few minutes earlier, when I was in the living room, he called out painfully, two times, "Help me, help me." As always, he wasn't sure what disturbed him, with no recollection he was yelling for help.

But this opened up a brief talk about this life and what follows. He told me, for the first time: "I have some fear for what will follow me from this life." In the past, more than once, he said he was ready for death and had no fear.

"Fear of what Mac?" But he couldn't or wouldn't say of what. As he lay there with his hands in prayer over his chest, I suggested again, "Mac, you really have nothing to fear."

He said, with a tone of sarcasm, "That's good to know." So, maybe, as someone suggested, to put his hands in a pray pose, was, non-verbal sarcasm. Mac was a good man, but mostly non-religious.

That evening, with only two days to go, it was my attempt to help him accept his transition. It was so, so, close. He was suffering—maybe afraid he will suffer in the next life also. He couldn't talk about it, even though I left it open for him.

Three a.m. that same night he called for help to go the bathroom. When he was back in bed he said one of his favorite expressions: "Oh, what a life we live."

"You're really stretching it out, Mac."

"Well, most people go through a process."

"Some leave tragically, like Steve, going real quick." Steve was a brother-in-law who was 90 years old and a very close friend. He and his wife, Jill, were killed a just few weeks earlier in a car accident.

In those last hours, Mac's mind was clear as he reminded me of talks we had about his friend's accident. "Steve was driving too fast at that curve. His foot probably slipped off the break onto the accelerator."

"You're probably right on that one."

"Bob, I think about the after life. I think it's pleasant."

"That's good Mac. Try and go to the light."

"What?"

"I've heard, when someone dies and they see the light—go to it."

"There's nothing to be afraid of. I hear it's pleasant."

"I've heard you say you're ready."

"I'm in the process."

"I think there's always a long line."

"Well, I'm waiting."

"Good night Mac, sleep well."

"Thanks Bob. You sleep well too."

The following day I was off.

The next day was my three-hour substitute shift for Lynn.

A small foot note: I didn't want to confuse the readers, but both Mac's name and Leo's name were Bob. Three Bob's.

# Short Notice

It was another one of those exceptional days at work that made me feel good being a medical social worker for a home care agency. Nurses who work for the same agency would give me my referrals. The nurses gave me information about patients who they had visited in the patients' home. Sometimes, the nurse felt there needed to be a social work visit because something was going on with the patient or the family other than their medical problems. After a couple of years of doing this work I came to appreciate the opportunity it gave me to do something worthwhile.

While driving to a patient's home my thoughts were about the referral and maybe my talk with the nurse about what I might encounter at the patient's home. There was also the consideration, and this was important to me, of what I was going to do to help the patient or family and satisfy something of the nurse's concern. At times my role was very matter of fact with the help I brought to the family or individual. Sometimes it was almost as if a power beyond myself was right there with me. This unseen power helps the words come out of my mouth. And what does come out is helpful to the patient and or family members. Sometimes, there was disappointment all around when there was nothing I could do to help.

On this day my referral was to visit an 83 year-old man who was diagnosed with brain cancer. Three weeks prior to his diagnosis, he was fine, without symptoms, or none he was acknowledging to others, or maybe to himself. The nurse told me the patient was feeling well enough to have made plans to travel to a car show in the Midwest. This is something he had been doing for many years. According to the nurses' referral, Sam began to have discomforting symptoms, dizziness and weakness, although with no pain. When he went for a medical exam he was told of the tumor. The doctors said that without treatment he would have only three to six months to live and even with treatment his quality of life was questionable.

An attractive woman answered the door of singlewide trailer in a rural area outside of Gainesville, Florida. I had previously made a phone call so she knew I was on my way. I introduced myself and told her, as I had on the phone, that the nurse had asked me to see Sam. She introduced herself as Sam's ex-wife. She also introduced me to Adele, their 13 year-old daughter.

"We should sit down," Judy began, "and talk before you go in to see Sam. He has a hard time communicating. Adele and I will fill you in on what's going on with Sam. What you should know about him is that he has been a very independent man most of his life. He was in vaudeville for many years and until recently he traveled all over the world as an entertainer.

"When we divorced I didn't want to move very far from where Sam lived so both of us could have contact with Adele. We also still wanted to see each other. One of his great qualities is that he is a good person. He did visit with me and Adele regularly when he was home."

I could sense right away, from how she discussed Sam, that for an ex-wife, Judy was very kind and obviously still cared about him.

Judy told me she had taken on the 24 hour seven days a week care for Sam since he very quickly became unable to do much for him self.

We only briefly touched on nursing home care as an option if he became too much for her. Because he weighed over 200 pounds, I reminded her, "Be very careful not to strain yourself as you move him around."

She laughed and said, "Thanks. Tell me about it. I'm very careful moving him around. So far I've managed without problems.

"Taking care of Sam is a big deal," she said. "I used to take care of my mother, so I know some of the day to day routine. My main concern, to be honest, is that Sam is very much in denial about the seriousness of his illness. He tells me daily, 'I'm going to get better,' and at times he tries to do things on his own."

"I hear that frequently about patients who are suddenly struck with a serious illness. It's hard to give up what we have been previously doing. What's even harder is to give up who we have been."

"I know," she followed up. "I try to imagine what he is going through. I like Sam. It's so hard for Adele and me to see him seriously ill. We have another major concern. He has totally refused to sign a living will. He told me if his condition eventually warrants life support intervention, that is what he wants."

"Did he tell you for how long?"

"Yes, I asked him, and he told me, smiling, 'for five years.'"

"Five years. Hmm. Was he a comedian as part of his vaudeville act? Maybe he was just joking."

"Yes he was a comedian, but he was quite serious about that." She confirmed this by asking, Adele, what she thought.

"Oh, yeah, I heard him say that too."

"Another problem," Judy continued, seemingly feeling comfortable with me and I sensed a bit desperate, "is that he was also refused to assign anyone to be his health care surrogate. To be honest with you Mr. Bob, I'm very distressed over what's going on with him. It's not only his illness, but also the denial, and his refusal to sign those important papers. He also hasn't signed a will about his estate. It's not a whole lot, but substantial. He has another daughter he has disowned due to her lifestyle. She will make hell for us if he dies and there's no will. I know you don't deal with all that, but I really need some help with him on these issues. I don't know what you can do. And the truth is four or five people have been here to talk with him about all of this. No one has gotten him to agree to anything."

"Have you told him you would be his health care surrogate?" I asked her.

"No, I don't want to do that. I can't. But he has another lady friend who said she would. She's a neighbor and they've been friendly."

"Well, okay ma'am, I'll give it a try. Do you think it's okay for me to talk to him about signing those papers?"

"Yes, please do. I hope you have better luck than the others."

It was a bit awkward, being a stranger and being asked to talk about very personal matters. On the other hand, I also believe that none of us are strangers. We are all part of the same stuff that makes up this life. I had trust in my skills of communication and honesty. Judy walked me into his bedroom, introduced me, and left.

"Hi Sam, your home care nurse asked me to come out and see you. I had a nice talk with Judy and your daughter. Judy told me about your work in vaudeville and that you had a road trip planned to see a car show."

I paused and waited, but all he did was look directly into my eyes. He seemed to acknowledge my talk, but only with barely discernable head nods.

"Judy also told me you understood everything going on with your recent diagnosis. She said you have been talking about it a bit." He just stared.

"I don't walk in your shoes Sam, but I am trying to understand how difficult the past few weeks have been since you received the diagnosis of inoperable brain cancer. I know the doctors recommended radiation treatments."

He still didn't acknowledge me verbally. He just continued to look directly at me with an occasional nod. No smiles, no change of expression. It was impossible for me to know whether to attribute this unresponsiveness to disinterest, to the tumor or quite possibly depression. I regretted not talking about this to Judy.

I breathed and went on trying to feel guidance from a higher power.

"I don't want to be probing into your life Sam, but in talking with Judy she gave me some sense of your intelligence and inner spirit."

It was touchy, but I began to feel more at ease, since he hadn't sent me away, turned his head or even closed his eyes.

"In doing this work Sam, and in reading and studying, I've gotten to understand a bit about life and death and the transient nature of our bodies. We're here and then were not. It's hard to give up this life. It's all we know." Again, he nodded slightly. "There's a chance you may get stronger after the radiation therapy which begins next week, but from what the doctors think, that may only gave give you a few more months or maybe a year at the most. The chances are Sam, you won't be even close to who you have been."

Judy told me he knew all this and understood the diagnosis. Apparently though, he hadn't accepted the prognosis. Like most of us, he wanted to hold on to the thin thread of life he still had.

"Judy told me that when you saw your mother dying some years ago, kept alive by medical technology, you told Judy, 'Never let this happen to me; take me out and shoot me.'" He nodded his head up and down.

Knowing how he felt before his own diagnosis, there was now some basis for where I was being led.

"From what Judy told me you have lived a full and enjoyable life." He nodded. Ah, another response.

"I have to ask you, did you really tell Judy you wanted

to remain on life support for five years?" I chuckled a bit, and had to add, "Were you serious, or were you being the comedian?"

At that he finally broke and laughed, his whole, jolly, plump body shook, but only said, "I just got out of the hospital."

"I know Sam." I paused. "To anyone it would be a great shock being told they have a terminal illness. But that is the reality." I paused again, breathed lightly, as he continued to stare into my eyes with a deadpan expression. "You know the doctors will have to make medical decisions for you if you went into a condition where you couldn't make them yourself." He nodded, understanding. "You really should have someone you trust, who knows what you want, assigned to help decide for you.

"Judy told me she didn't want to do that. How about the other lady friend Judy told me about?"

He again said, "I just got out of the hospital."

Later, as I was leaving, Judy told me that was all he said when anyone talked with him about this issue.

"I understand Sam, but you also have an estate. Judy told me you have no will. You know it would be a mess if you didn't put something on paper. Your loved ones need to know what you want them to have when that time comes. Judy told me about your older daughter who you don't want to have anything and you've disowned. While you still have your intelligence, you should take care of this. Adele told me your older daughter would fight for part of your possessions and your estate. I don't deal with that stuff, but it is something you should take care of soon." He again nodded.

Then, out of blue: "Do you want me to sign something?"

I was taken aback, but said, "Only if you understand what I'm talking about." He nodded and said, "Yes, I do." I showed him the paper. He was reading the newspaper when I came in to see him and Judy and Adele were certain he could still read and understand.

I needed to be careful not to be pushy; after all, it was about his life. To help a person get ready to die is no small matter. It is my work, but to deal with life and death is more than a job. In those moments, my feeling is, I'm in a position of being one with the Beloved. It's the High Work of life. I showed him the papers and he glanced through them. I asked him: "Do you want food and water withheld if death is near and the doctor's don't expect you to live without them?" He quietly said, "Yes." I asked him again if he understood what that means. Again he quietly said, "Yes," and reached for the pen in my hand. He signed the living will, than signed the paper assigning the other woman to be his health care surrogate.

At that moment the physical therapist from our agency came into his room to do some work with him. There wasn't much she could do except try and keep his body as limber as he was able during those remaining months. We talked a bit as I watched her work with Sam for a few minutes. My work was done. I got up from my chair and walked to his bed. When I reached out my hand he put his hand out and shook mine with a strong grip looking straight into my eyes. "I really enjoyed this bit of time with you Sam, and appreciate the difficult time you're having."

There was a slight twinge of wonder in me if he

questioned what we had done together. After we let go of each other hands, I watched the physical therapist work with him a few more minutes as she checked his range of motion with his arms and legs. "Sam I'll see you next week at the cancer clinic."

I went into the living room with Judy and Adele spending a few minutes sharing with them what went on with Sam. While listening to her comments about all the others who had tried to get him to sign the papers I felt thankful being able to accomplish what we did together. There was a bit of wonderment about this life of mine. Maybe he was tired of hearing the same routine or was just tired, or maybe something else.

Sometimes in going off to do this work there's a feeling deep inside of me that the Universe has sent me on an assignment. Laughing to myself there is gratitude this really is the case. This is good work, with pay, but I still know there is another level of life going on. There is an intention beyond self, of actually being an instrument, a Co-creator, with the Divine. There is a belief in me, that on some level, all life is co-creating together some people putting out more intention than others.

Sam didn't come in for radiation treatment the following week. The nurse told me he was still deciding what to do. A few weeks later she told me he was getting weaker fast and didn't have much time left.

## Hester's Last Smile
## and Can of Rolling Tobacco

In the nursing home where I work people are dying regularly. Most of the dying are elderly. But sometimes people are being admitted, in their forties and fifties, who are terminally ill with one critical illness or another. All are destitute; that's why they're in this nursing home. We will accept the poorest of the poor. Don't get misled though—we aren't taking them because of some idealistic humanitarian concern. The fact is we are the oldest and least sought after home in town. We take the people no one else will accept.

In many cases, what brought these younger folks into the nursing home is some of their own doing. We could lay their problem on poor decision-making. Sure, we're told we all have free will. But when life doesn't get us off in the right direction, many times life can go astray, and never get us back on track. We tend to blame the person for living a poor lifestyle, making wrong decisions. Ha! Not ha, funny, but a laugh of derision for the inequities that life thrusts on so many. Maybe, in their entire lives, they never had the opportunity to know what right decision making was. Sure, we're all responsible for our own lives, but what if someone was never able to get a decent life going. The causes are legion. We all know of the stories of abuse or how a person was raised or growing up in poverty or mental instability. Sometimes there is generalized ignorance of what someone eats, drinks, smokes, etc. Did they have a chance? And sometimes the will to change is not there or the causes are so inculcated what chance did they have?

Then at some point they are too far-gone for anyone to shake them awake and tell them to get their lives on track. The only track is chronic illness, which may be leading them to an early end-of-life stage.

As the social worker, I'm given the opportunity to offer some last ditch effort of help. But help with what? Getting social services is usually tricky and sometimes difficult considering the Draconian system that has been devised for all those in need. Because of many years doing this work, I've become good at working the system and getting what people need. But now I'm thrust into an environment where some of what I help people do is die—if that is something any of us can really do for another. The least I can do is be there with them with love, compassion and understanding offering a bit of guidance in what might be next.

It has been a good learning for me to feel love and give support to people I've only recently met. But before accessing those love energies I needed to raise my ability to feel for another. This came to me through many years of yogic breathing practices and spiritual teachings. This has allowed me to receive and send love—the primary healing ingredient.

In all the ways of knowing about myself, this tuning of myself was with me before I knew it was there. It involved meditations and prayers, trying to attune to all the seen and unseen beings that are with me. Early in my adulthood there was something in me that was unmet—a yearning to be in touch with an unseen, mystical world. Tuning myself into spirit helped guide me in the stories in this book. Over the years as my spiritual life continued to unfold, I became more in touch with those intuitive energies.

Hester, in her mid fifties, is dying of cancer. She was more or less a street woman who off and on usually had a place to stay. She was known at the local shelter (not far from the nursing home) where she came in occasionally for a meal or needing a bed for the night. As a younger woman, she worked, had a husband and children. Now she only knows one 18-year-old daughter who has been coming to visit.

"When did you see your other children," I asked her? She tries to whisper something to me. When she can't get the words out because her tracheotomy is clogged with mucous, she puts up ten thin fingers, makes a fist and holds them up again.

"Twenty years?" I ask her. She smiles and nods.

I've taken to Hester because she reminds me of a woman I went with many years ago. Both were alcoholics. The woman I knew died at 50, of general dissipation. The throat cancer in Hester has metastasized throughout her abdomen. This is putting her in excruciating pain. The pain is being lessened by strong doses of pain medications ordered by her hospice nurse and doctor. None of it though seems enough to deaden her discomfort. Very soon she will have an I.V. Morphine pump. She will then be able to administer to herself with the self-regulating pump. It will most likely be enough to deaden all her pain and eventually ease her out of this life.

Hester is tiny—90 pounds. Although there are many rooms in this nursing home, her room is right next to my office. It allowed me a more frequent connection making it so easy to visit. I appreciated where she was placed—on the other side of a thin wall.

This morning when I go in to visit she is sitting on the side of her bed. Hester's head is down, hanging limply towards her stomach. Her legs are crunched up under her as she tries to find a position that is comfortable: Any position to lessen the pain. Of all the dying people I have worked with, Hester is one I want to especially help. There is only a little to do though; sit with her, offer comforting words, touch her hand, rub her head or neck, invite a student massage therapist to very, very gently work on her.

I take her hand and cup it in mine while sitting on her bed. She tries to explain something to me. The tracheotomy is constantly dripping thick, stringy, yellow, mucous she wipes with tissues. The tissues are collecting on her bed, some gather in a pile on the floor. Later some one picks them up. The hospice nurse calls the dripping mucous bronchitis. When Hester can't talk due to the mucous, she asks for her notebook. She tries to write messages with her uneducated spelling. It's her own phonetic language: some words almost unintelligible.

But she writes. She even seems to like writing. I think of suggesting she do more, except now, with only a few weeks to go, she is barely able to hold the pen.

This is her second time coming to the nursing home. Hester was with us four months ago for a few weeks. Then she went back to her apartment trying to make a go of it on her own with friends helping. She walked in the first time. This time, she was only able to walk holding on to the back of a wheelchair. Somehow she managed to carry two large cans of a cheap rolling tobacco, one tucked under each arm. Very quickly, sooner then anyone thought, after only a few days, she needed to sit in the wheelchair and be pushed onto the patio so she could have another cigarette. No more walking.

The picture of her awkwardly pushing the wheelchair with the rolling tobacco under her arms is still with me. I pointed at her coming down the hall and gave her a friendly welcome laugh. She laughed back knowing she presented a different kind of picture. In the confusion of coming back to the nursing home in her weakened condition, she misplaced one can on the second day. I found it in the staff break room and she agreed to let me hold it in my office.

What am I to do for her? Get down on my hands and knees and pray that she doesn't have too much pain? The morphine will take care of that. Should I ask God to help her go fast? She is on her way from this life. Hester told me a few times she's ready to die, especially with all the pain.

I want her to have a chance. A chance that when she dies and faces the hungry and deceitful demons (a

Buddhist term referring to unconscious impressions) she confronted in life she can allow them to pass her by so she can see some light of goodness. Maybe she can make amends, come back around again, with some opportunity to live a decent life.

What can we really known about dying? I have read Buddhists teachings, Jewish teachings, the Christian teachings, Sufi teachings and others. There is wonderment in me about those mystical teachings of living and dying that have been passed on to me. I reach deep within myself trying to understand as best I can this mystery we live.

Within her are hints of a latent spirituality. Maybe they are in all of us. I bring up God and she tries to explain something. Then reaches for the notebook and writes about God. Three years ago she found herself seeking. Hester looks in my eyes, shrugs her bony, thin-skinned shoulders as if to say, "What does it all mean anyway?"

Her nightgown comes away, exposing her flattened, wrinkled breasts. When I cover her she smiles, shrugs, knowing it makes no difference. Maybe she's lived a full life and doesn't have to come back for any more turns in human existence. I suggest, in as kind of voice as possible, "When you pass from this plane, if you sees the light, try and go with it. Be with the light." She nods, understanding a little. Maybe one needn't be a saintly person. Maybe she experienced more of life then anyone needs to live. Maybe she learned and knows something about life that can carry her to the light. In my work I try to draw something out of her that can give her solace as she prepares to enter the other side.

My wonder: if I'll ever see her smile again. Her head is hanging low, down to her abdomen as she nods, eyes closed, in a stupor on the strong pain meds.

Later she is sitting outside on the patio with the other smokers limply holding a long-ashed cigarette in her emaciated fingers. Her breathing gargles through her tracheotomy.

Hester still has a pretty face, but now it's too much of a wrinkled face; like her breasts, closer to a 70 year-old than a woman in her fifties.

Her few teeth are black and rotten. Still, her smile is somehow bright and frequent. Sometimes when at home I wonder will I ever see it again? I've gotten attached to her. It's impossible to breathe any more life into her than what I have and it isn't enough. It will be slow and painful. The hospice nurse promises me again, Hester will soon be on the morphine pump. She'll be able to give herself as much as she can take.

The hospice social worker and I agreed we should make arrangements with a local mortuary for her requested cremation. It won't cost Hester anything. I asked her if she wants me to spread her remains on Payne's Prairie; the 1000s of acres of natural, pristine Florida. A favorite place of mine where one can be with many birds, see alligators, giant turtles, herons, mushrooms, deer, transplanted buffalo and wild horses. The Prairie is right down the road from the nursing home. She nodded she did, whispering, "I've been there."

I think about her turning to ash, which is more like gritty rough sand. Unburned bone. Now here she sits in front of me, but some time soon, all that will be left of her physical being will be unburned bone. I'm mystified: We go from what I see now in front of me. Then, the unseen, mystery part, spirit, energy, soul, goes off to somewhere unknown to most of us.

It was easy to laugh to myself about being a crazed dervish man from another time, here now, waiting and helping and being with Hester. In less than three years I have already been with dozens of dying. This has been my work: The Creator's work given to me. My choice to do this for Creator since Life, I reckon, is Me, and Me is Life, and Hester, is also a part of That. I am going to help dispose of what is left of her body when she no longer breathes in the life force.

What do I know that she doesn't? All my praying and studying and meditating make me someone much different from who she is. But we are all part of the One, brought here together, to this place, this nursing home, so the staff can do something for her: To help her along. I still wonder if anyone really needs to be helped along in their dying. Oh yes—according to the "Tibetan Book of Living and Dying" there is work to be done to help the dying, Maybe it's enough: Just being with her and supporting her, praying for her, and letting her know she won't be alone. "You won't be alone," are the words that came out of me today. How will I know when she is about to die? What if I'm at home? The staff can call me if they have a feel for her last hour, her last moments. Sometimes we know. I've known.

Frequently, the staff gets sensitive to that moment. We tell one another. It gets passed around so those who care can go in the room and spend a few last sacred moments with someone they worked with, helped along, in and out of bed, administered medication, changed dressings, spoon fed, cleaned up all fluids that come out of a sick, dying person.

The thoughts of a madman: I'm sitting on her bed imagining doing like I've seen junkies do, tying off my arm and melting down heroin. Taking a syringe and watch the white-grey liquid going up into it. Clenching my fist so a nice vein pops up real good. Then shooting up as she pumps the morphine into her vein and we nod off together. I think of the two bottles of vodka in my office desk that I took out of Hester's dresser after a nurse told me about them. Hester told me to take them. She said they weren't hers but belonged to a friend. What am I supposed to believe?

"Are you going through any alcohol withdrawal, do you need these bottles close to you?" She looks at me surprised and denies alcohol was the problem, as she brings two fingers to her mouth mimicking taking a puff of a cigarette.

She's has done her share of drinking. Her good friend, Jo Ann, comes to see her regularly to give Hester a bath. Only two weeks ago, Hester was getting into Jo Ann's pick-up and going back to her apartment to complete some things there. Jo Ann tells me Hester really enjoyed her vodka, even put some in coffee in the morning to get her day going. Jo Ann, who knows Hester for two years, tells me that Hester owes nothing to life: She has lived it fully. My thoughts are on Hester's bottles off and on, wondering if her friend, if there really is a friend, doesn't come for the bottles, should I indulge myself and drink up the innocent-looking throat-burning liquid in commemoration to Hester after she dies. It is odd for me to think this way—heroin and vodka? It's never been my way, but never have I felt this way about someone.

Will she be the last dying person I care for in the nursing home? Maybe quit after this is over with Hester, and agree with myself that this has been enough: I've done the work given to me; enough is enough, let me get on with other work that is fun. Let me have another lighter way to go for the remainder of my workdays. It's impossible to keep track how many times I've had this thought. Six decades of life, more than half of them as a social worker. What more is there for me to do? How many lives must I help along the way, in trying to ease their path? Have I been cheating, not suffering as much as the many I have helped? Is this, some kind of guilt or redemption trip my life has been on, atoning for known and unknown malevolence in this life of mine.

My life, though, has been mostly benevolent living being brought to do the work of a helper. One day a few years ago, while riding to work to see an abused, emotionally disturbed adolescent girl I had worked with for a couple of years, a realization came to me: My life was like a modern day shaman, going from home to home, town to town, program to program, agency to agency, ministering in the guise of a social worker. Odd, thinking of all the time spent berating myself for not making more money, not being something else, not being successful, while all along, doing the Great Work. Who knew? No one told me when I began on this path there was even a path—that it would be my Life's Path. It was the Great

Work, not a business, with all the scheming and conniving. I used to think that business was the hardball league, one I didn't fit into. It always made more sense, slow pitching, not having to try and compete or get over on someone as in a business arrangement. Traveling the shaman path, trying to figure out how to make someone else's life trip less traumatic, easing pain, softening the burdens, but accepting there may never be solutions. I understood that from my own life. Life is relentless, constantly coming at us. We work through it as part of the trip—it is the life. As a middle-aged retarded man told me, "Life is life." Through his small vision of life there was a bit of simple, but grand wisdom. There is no getting away from it.

For now: still here with Hester. A few days later, she's very morphined out. She can barely sit up. She's barely taking anything to drink. Hester hasn't really eaten much in the four weeks she's been with us. Now her eyes are closed most of the time. She has occasional tremors, grimaces on her face, no smiles, except a very slight, corner of the mouth smile, when the hospice nurse got real close to her face and made a joke.

A homeless waif, Carolyn, who knew Hester in the St. Francis House homeless shelter, is sitting on the next bed to Hester as the hospice nurse and I talk with Hester. Carolyn has been coming in and spending her days with Hester. She bargains with the staff for a couple of nights of sleep on an empty bed next to Hester and some meals. But soon she began demanding from us: regular meals, a nightly bed. We had to let her know she can't be spending nights here and we don't feed people. She quickly became an irritant to the staff, as she wanted to know "How come you don't have a feeding tube in Hester? How come you're not trying to feed her more and how come you're not trying to save her?" How come this, how come that? The hospice staff, with my help, went over and over with Carolyn about Hester's situation. She didn't get it.

The staff becomes more aware Carolyn had some serious emotional problems. Her own needs were more the priority than Hester's. I hoped she would understand we are doing our best to make it right for Hester.

But Carolyn couldn't grasp what we were doing to help Hester. She began whispering to Hester she should have a feeding tube and I.V. liquids so she will live. One morning, coming into work a nurse told me she had to call hospice to tell them Hester now wants those heroic measures. None of us believed that was what Hester wanted. We would have to give them to her if she asked for them. I went into Hester's room and Carolyn was sitting there. She wouldn't look at me, or answer my "Good morning" to her. I made my own call to the hospice nurse, leaving a message that she has to come in and have a talk with Hester. Late in the morning the hospice nurse came in and we discussed the situation regarding Carolyn. At my suggestion the hospice nurse went in alone to see Hester. Carolyn walked out going past my doorway still ignoring me when I try to get her attention. Later the staff talked about rumors Carolyn threatened to call the state elder abuse hot line to report the nursing home. It's a little extra drama added to an already delicate situation.

Hester's 18-year-old daughter, Leola, was in the room with Hester. She has been spending a lot of time with Hester the past two days. She signed the "do not resuscitate order" for her mother two days earlier, at the request of Hester. If her heart stops she does not want CPR. Leola is very much out of her element—nursing home, dying mother, signing papers, her own two-year-old son. She is trying to have power of attorney over Hester's measly bank account. She is a strong young woman, dealing with things as best as she can. Maybe she's making up for time they didn't spend together. I talked with her a day earlier needing to know about the relationship she had with her mother. She tells me, "I was taken away from my Mom by the state and put in foster homes when I was 11 because of Mom's drinking. I spent some time with my father after the foster homes, but never lived with Hester again." Actually, they had only seen each other a few times in the ensuing years. Now they are making up for lost mother and daughter time by the attention they are giving to each other. Leola brings her two-year-old son with her regularly so Hester can enjoy the company of her grandson.

The hospice nurse is in the room for about 20 minutes. I go in and catch the tail end of the nurse explaining to Hester and Leola that because of her very weak condition if the feeding tubes were put in, her body might react by the lungs getting clogged with liquids and she would aspirate. There didn't seem to be any benefit for this procedure. Fortunately, Hester has been more alert this morning than all week. I was surprised earlier in the day someone left her sitting in a wheelchair outside my office. When I asked her if she wanted to go out onto the patio, she nodded yes. I pushed her out there where she sat for a while, surprisingly with no cigarette.

For two days in a row, Hester has been more alert, sitting up, enjoying the time with Leola and her grandson. Her body is getting used to the morphine. I joke with her about missing her own baptism. It happened while she was mostly in a sleepy drugged state, after being introduced to the morphine pump. She previously indicated she wanted to be baptized and a Catholic priest came in and performed the sacred ritual. The priest answered all the questions he put to Hester himself. I had never seen this ritual before. I wondered how he could answer for someone else about whether they are rejecting Satan, and accepting God. It was later explained to me that that's how it's done so even people in a coma can be saved. I am satisfied with myself not judging other religious traditions.

Hester's is only sipping a bit of the nutritional supplements we keep offering her. She also takes a sip of water now and then. She can't go on for too long. Each day when I spend time with her, she keeps asking me, 'When? How much longer?' I tell her, "You just have to wait your turn. There are others ahead of you." She surprised me as she looked deeply into my eyes, nodding she understood. The eye connection we are having is leaving a deep, and forever-lasting impression on me. And now, in this moment, there's a realization—that so many of those who I helped in the nursing home, helping with their transition from this life, and for all of us, whoever we are with, part of them become us. We them, as our life is literally transformed from each and every experience we are having in this life. We are becoming all that has been in our lives.

I would spend more time with Hester, if time were available. There are 90 other residents in this nursing home with only one social worker. I walk out of Hester's room and talk with Judy, 58, who is going through a long, slow cancerous process, then a talk with Nelson, 56, out on the back patio smoking as usual. I've appreciated myself for being able to help this once-homeless man. Working the system I helped get him on disability and Medicaid, then cataract surgery, dentures and a spinal operation after all his limbs were becoming numb. With some hesitation, hoping I wasn't jumping ahead of things, I offer him the last can of Hester's rolling tobacco. It's been in my office desk drawer. He tells me "Thanks, I'll come get it later."

I sat in Hester's room yesterday watching her twitch and wiggle around a bit. She looked pitifully weak and done with this life. Off and on she would open her eyes a crack, and look at me, but she wasn't able, nor was it necessary for her to acknowledge my presence. I patted her on the hand, rested my hand on her forehead for a few moments. Then brushed back her hair with my fingers. I whispered to her, "Hester it looks like it won't be much longer." There was no response, except when I asked her if she wanted a blanket or sheet she mouthed, "Sheet." Covering her, it almost felt like I needed to cover her face. She was getting that close. One more prayer hoping she didn't have to continue her ordeal much longer.

When I came to work the next morning they were wheeling her body past my office, just in time for one last good-bye. Leola will take her mom's remains to a place they both care about.

## We Won't Forget —
## Pete's Home Is in the Woods

Pete was almost always with a smile and a friendly hello when we came in to see him at this campsite in the woods. He usually had a cigarette between his dirty stained fingers with a beer in his other hand. He sat on his porch swing near his tents. Set firmly on his head was a felt, western style hat, the brim curved above his ears with Spanish moss wrapped around the high crown. He had a small stuffed snoopy dog sitting on top, and an American Flag on one side. There was a Hooter's emblem on the front. Under the hat, a long ponytail hung down in back, with a narrow bearded face and piercing, blue eyes in front. He always had wise cracking language that kept others smiling.

On my first visit to his homeless camp, I was immediately drawn to the creek that passed ten feet from his tent. It was Sweetwater Branch that ran lazily through town picking up pollutants as it meandered to Payne's Prairie loosing itself in a sinkhole. I didn't know Pete at all, but an appreciation swept through me, seeing him living in this place in the woods by a creek.

After being introduced to him by one of the Home Van crew I sat down next to him, on the old porch swing. Others talked about him so fondly I hoped he would know me a bit better when I saw him again. "Hey Pete, it looks like you're set up good here by the creek. I hope you don't mind me asking, but have you been here very long?"

He turned and looked at me square in the eyes: "Yeah, it's been a while," then turned back to the cold fire pit in front of the porch swing that had seen better days.

"I like your spot here. Near the creek."

"Yeah, it's a good one."

Arupa who knew Pete and most of the homeless in the camps and around town, came up to Pete, "Pete how you feeling?"

"Hey Ms Arupa, I'm hanging in there. Gonna listen to the Gator game on Saturday. I hope my batteries hold out. May have to get some new ones before Saturday."

"Hey, Pete," I interjected, "if you need batteries, I can bring some out to you."

"No thanks," uh, what's you name?"

"Sh'mal. I have time and don't mind."

"No, I appreciate it, but I gotta bike into town to get beer before Saturday. What'dya say your name was?"

"Sh'mal. You'll get it after a while. I'm going to be a regular with the Home Van."

"Hey, if you're helping with Ms Arupa, you must be okay. Ms Arupa, thanks for the sandwiches and soup and stuff. It always helps."

"You're welcome Pete," Arupa, responded. We love coming by to see you. Everything been okay."

"I heard the police have been chasing people out of some of the camping places."

"Yeah, they have. No one is sure what to do about it. After a while we get fed up talking to the City Commissioners. They don't give a shit since the downtown business people want you all out of town. Hey, we gotta move along. We'll see you next week."

"Thanks again for dropping off the food and soup."

"We'll see you next week. Love you Pete."

"Love you too Ms Arupa. He stood up and gave Arupa a hug, ignoring me as I said, "See you soon Pete."

The four of us walked out of his campsite back up the hill to pass out some more of the food we had this evening.

I sensed a slight uncomfortable incongruence in myself; I was bringing him food, yet feeling or sensing he had something to give me. My friends and I and the world at large referred to those living in the woods as homeless, but seeing Pete with his unique set up, it didn't look like he was homeless. It looked like a home to me.

That first day—it felt like an honor.

One week later, as others brought food to camps further in the woods, I carried Pete his food. It wasn't much but the homeless folks living outside of town appreciated the sandwich, soup, bottled water, snack, banana, whatever donated food we had that week. It was a 50-yard narrow path through the woods to his camp off the dead end where we parked the van. I called out announcing, "Home Van coming in." It was like knocking on a door, our way of letting folks know some one was approaching their campsites. The sun was back near the end of the day spreading moving shadows through the trees. There was uncertainty in me about my motives to those I was meeting, but trusting something within of wanting to offer help to others. When I saw Pete's camp, he was sitting on his swinging lounge seat, cigarette between fingers, beer on the round log table in front of him. The fire pit was smoldering a bit.

"Hey doctor." He gave me a smile.

"I'm not a doctor. I'm a social worker."

"I know," he said, with a friendly smile through brown, rotting, teeth. "Here's a beer?"

"Sure. Your camp looks good Pete, being close to the creek. Reminds me of places I camped as a kid. It feels relaxed. How long you been here?"

"Been here a few years."

I sipped my beer, with the thought of living in the woods. "I don't think I could do this."

"Probably not."

"Where else you been living?"

"Oh here and there. A few years outside of Atlanta. When I got out of the service, after Nam, I went back home to New York State, but it was too friggin cold up there."

"Yeah, know what you mean. I grew up in New Jersey, but lived all over the country. I love living in Gainesville."

He told me he just turned 60; another Viet Nam vet, who just didn't want to, or maybe couldn't, deal with the usual way of life most of us try to fit into.

Pete was one of the regulars on our two times a week route to the homeless camps around Gainesville. We always enjoyed the stop at Pete's camp since the Home Van regulars had made Pete a bit of an icon, giving him an honored place due to his age and individualistic nature.

About a year after I met Pete he began to get sick. He was getting thinner and thinner. The Home Van cadre who had visited him the past few years could see something was seriously wrong. When he finally told us he couldn't swallow so well, we understood a little better what was going on. To help him a bit we began to bring him nutritional supplements. He told us he liked them, but we thought it odd that we never saw any empty cans in his small garbage pile next to his tents. Only beer cans. Although we couldn't get the supplements all the time due to expense and shortage of donated money, we felt we needed to add something to this mainly beer diet.

Pete had his campsite away from the other homeless campsites. He wasn't interested in living near the others, but wouldn't chase anyone from his area if they set up camp and didn't cause any problems. He was set up good, with the 7 by 7 tent he slept in and two small storage tents behind his main one. He usually had a transistor radio playing country and western music when we came to see him. He also had a battery operated TV with a two inch screen he could get local football games and the weather. Blackie his cat was usually near by, and a rifle always leaning against his sleeping tent. Of all the homeless sites, his was the only one with a displayed weapon, although some carried knives in sheaths on their hips. Pete said he had the rifle in case snakes or raccoons come close to the camp and bothered Blackie.

The regular volunteers of our Home Van cadre, who saw Pete weekly, discussed his situation as we did others, for who we had concerns.

"What should we do about Pete's throat problem?" I

asked. "What have you done in the past when others were sick?" Even after a year I was still the new guy.

Arupa, said, "We've taken a few to the E.R. when some one has something that isn't going away. I have a feeling his condition is more serious. You worked as the social worker Sh'mal, what do you think?"

"I don't know. Is there a doctor that you know?"

"Yeah, you're right, there is a doctor that used to come out with us sometimes. I'll give him a call."

We all loved Pete; in his way, he was a special person we cared about and wanted to help. Maybe him being a rebel amongst the other rebels or maybe there was something primal that we looked for in ourselves.

Pete progressively became worse. He told us he was spitting up blood and had a still harder time swallowing. There was now a lump protruding near his Adams apple and his voice was getting weaker. None good signs, but Pete, being the rebel he was, refused to see any medical person. Finally, after we kept bugging him, he agreed to see Dr. John who Arupa called. John had recently resumed coming out with the Home Van to check on homeless people who couldn't afford medical care and had no insurance.

I discussed the lumps with John and he concurred that it could be cancer. Arupa, the woman who started the Home Van, brought Dr. John to Pete's campsite where he left a prescription for antibiotics. He told us, "They probably won't do any good, but for now, he can try these. He really needs to go to the E.R." I filled the prescription and brought it out to Pete.

"Hey, thanks, Doctor."

"Social worker, Pete."

"Yeah, I know. With that white beard and being a social worker, you're like a doctor."

"Well, not quite Pete, but I like helping you out." Pete took the pills regularly for the 10 days. He still had the lump and told us it was harder and harder to swallow food. At some point we began to notice two lumps. No one called them tumors around Pete. We were getting more concerned.

In order to win him over a bit and gain more trust, I brought a six-pack to his camp one afternoon. Actually, Arupa asked me to go and spend time with him. The beer was my idea. I almost never drink anything, but make exceptions. We sat and chatted. Mostly about sports, weather, living in the woods. It was a mission for me to try and gain Pete's confidence in what we were regularly suggesting for him to see a doctor at the E.R. It wasn't easy for me to talk about the growths by his throat, but it needed to be done.

"Pete, I know you know what's growing in your throat is not good."

"Yeah, I do. The stuff the doc gave me helped, but it's feeling worse. Now there are two."

"Yeah, we all see that. It really ain't good."

"Sh'mal, bring out a horse doctor."

"Sorry, Pete they don't visit the campsites anymore."

After a couple of back and forth lines about the growths, I had to say it. In a gentle caring voice, "You know Pete, it could be cancer."

He hesitated, "You think it might?"

"Well, I'm not a doctor, but I've been around medical

stuff for years and it could be. Arupa and the rest of us really think you should go to the hospital for a good exam. The E.R. A quick visit: I'll take you in."

"Well, I don't know maybe. We'll see."

Pete finally agreed, to our gentle but firm prodding. Dr. John made an appointment at the hospital. I was to be the escort.

As I'm driving down to get him at his camp I see him standing on Main Street smoking, leaning on his bike. After making a u-turn I pulled along side the curb. "Hey Pete, we're supposed to be going to the hospital for the exam. I came to get you."

"Yeah, yeah. I know." He wasn't irritated, maybe annoyed; he remained polite. "Thanks for coming to get me, I'm feeling much better, can talk now, no blood. Them pills the doc sent out really got rid of the problem."

It didn't surprise me. That was Pete. It was hard to imagine that the problem had gone, but listening to him was easy. It made no sense to try and persuade Pete to do anything. We just could encourage him. Pete was set up just where he wanted. He left no room for discussion. He'd been telling us for a while: "I'd rather die right here in the woods where I've been living for so long, or," smiling his smile, "see a horse doctor."

I joked with him more than once about horse doctors not coming out to the woods to see homeless vets. "It ain't happening Pete."

He smiled. "Sh'mal I was all set to go with you and then I thought about hospitals and changed my mind, as quick as that," snapping his fingers. He thanked me a few times for coming to get him. "No thanks when it comes to hospital procedures. Sorry you had to come looking for me."

"Well, who knows what they're going to do Pete, but I'm okay, if you're okay. We'll see ya on Thursday." I drove off with him weakly smiling and a wave. It was one of those instances that stay imprinted in memory.

Pete knew he was getting weaker. Arupa, along with me, finally persuaded him to apply for an apartment in a low-income senior building. I've taken Pete on as a friend and someone maybe we can help.

I helped him fill out the papers from the Housing Authority and advocated by having a meeting with the management to discuss his situation. The meeting helped since we only had to wait a week before we had an appointment with the manager who took us on a tour through the apartment. It was a pleasant surprise and a bit encouraging to see Pete with a constant smile of appreciation on his face as he looked around the one room efficiency with kitchenette and bathroom.

"Pete, you should have done this years ago."

"You're right Sh'mal, I'm getting too old for the woods."

This was a refrain he'd been chanting lately. He wasn't too old, just too weak and too debilitated. As we were looking around he was feeling good about the apartment. But my thought was, "we were too late." I didn't want the thought, but it came anyway. It was like knowing something I didn't want to know.

A couple of weeks later, Pete was barely coming out of his tent, and when he did he was literally crawling. It broke our hearts when Arupa and I knelt outside his tent and watched him crawl around inside putting on pants to come out and see us. We kept asking him, low key like, with no pressure, about going to the E.R. but he refused. It's his life.

One day though, when we were at his campsite, he surprised us, "Sh'mal come get me on Saturday." He was real clear, not asking. He told me. Arupa and I agreed to take him to the hospital on Saturday. Why Saturday we didn't know, but he chose the day.

When we showed up, we were prepared for a change of plans, but he was ready. He was in his usual garb of tight crusty jeans, plaid western shirt and the cowboy hat with all his fixings. He wasn't wearing his customary cowboy boots, but worn out sneakers. He said they were easier to get on and off. All his clothes were old and worn, but what he had on were his cleanest. Arupa was annoyed for not bringing him cleaner clothes.

At the emergency room, sensing his weakened condition, the nurses had us bypass the waiting room and put him directly in an examining room. This surprised me since some hospital staff weren't so kind to those who appear homeless. It was a long wait to be seen, but Pete was actually patient. Maybe he knew it was time to find out what was going on. We brought him coffee and he went out for a cigarette or two every hour or so. I wondered if he was admitted about withdrawal from his beer and cigarette addictions.

After a couple of nurses spoke with him and us, a doctor came in to do an exam. He felt the tumors in his neck. Then: "Pete you know what they might be," he abruptly, coldly, asked? I was surprised at his tone. Pete didn't respond. The doctor questioned him twice more, same question, same tone, but Pete was acting dumb, or afraid to respond. Or maybe, ah, this just came to me, as I write years later: Maybe in hearing the derisive tone of the doctor, why would anyone want to answer?

The young doctor blurts it out: "It's probably cancer and it'll probably kill you." That's it, perfect bedside manner to a poor homeless man on Medicaid. Would he have been so callous to a paying patient in a suit? Because I was a volunteer at the hospital as a non-denominational Chaplain, I maintained my demeanor and didn't express my shock at the doctor's attitude. I was surprised at my self-control, uncertain if I was being my authentic self. The doctor wasn't right. In fact he shouldn't be a doctor. It crosses my mind to tie him up and take him to the woods; lay him on a mound of fire ants, but Buddhist teachings prevail not allowing violence in my life. I wimp out and don't say anything. They have an ethics committee. I can report him.

Knowing how things work in a hospital, I get an Advanced Directive form that is needed so Pete can let the hospital staff know what interventions he doesn't want done. He was very clear that he didn't want any invasive treatments. Arupa and I assured him from the beginning we wouldn't allow it. He assigned Arupa and me to be his health care surrogates. This would allow us to make decisions for him. We also witnessed the form, making the form not legal. We can't be both, so I discard it, figuring once admitted the hospital staff would have him fill out the Advanced Directive form. It's supposed to be standard procedure.

Pete did get admitted and we told him we'd see him later. He was not acting nervous, but it was easy to sense him being uncomfortable; after all, from the woods to hospital. "I'll see you later in the evening Pete." He'll need support. That's my role.

When I came back in the evening he was in bed, awake and alert. We talked again about what treatments he didn't want done. I asked a nurse to come to his room so he could hear what Pete's wishes were in case he needed invasive treatment. He remained adamant: shaking his head vigorously, "No." He told the nurse very clearly he wanted none of the hospital technology. The nurse promised to put it in his notes so a doctor could sign an order to that effect. I was doing my share to help Pete through a difficult ordeal. Walking out of the hospital my thinking mind goes someplace else. Why can't I keep my mind focused? This was major event in Pete's life. In Arupa's and my life. I went home feeling woozy, tired, and ready for prayer-meditation and sleep.

The next morning there was a phone call from the hospital: Pete aspirated, choking on pureed foods or pudding or something they gave him. I didn't hear everything the nurse told me. He is on a ventilator, a breathing machine along with a feeding tube in his nose to his stomach. I'm shocked, flipped out a bit and quickly became irritated expressing my ire to the nurse, who was only the messenger. I told her, "I'll be there shortly."

When I drove to the hospital my mind raced around. I remembered I hadn't done my sitting meditation practice and morning breath work. "Pete, Pete," I mumble out loud in the car, sending prayers. Driving, I paid attention to my breath with some wonder and dread. What circumstances was I going to find at the hospital?

Before going to see Pete I made a quick stop in the volunteer office at the hospital to talk with Constance, the volunteer coordinator. I needed to tell her the situation, with a quick mention of yesterdays doctor in the E.R. She was extremely supportive knowing me as a volunteer Chaplin. She reassured me they would help. She called the patient representative who listened to the story and accompanied me to the medical intensive care unit. I appreciated the support, but already knew their help would be limited.

When we came into the medical intensive care unit, I saw Pete with how the nurse described him over the phone. There were tubes of various fluids/medications going into and out of him. I could see his hands tied to the bed rails because he was probably pulling on the tubes.

My friend Pete, who didn't want anything done to him, was getting everything modern medical technology can offer to keep him alive.

I'm irate, but maintain dignity; after all, after all what? Jumping up and down and screaming won't help. No, I'm an adult. I didn't want to be an adult; not then. Emotions, my ire, came out in my words, to a doctor, nurses, and a social worker about what the nurse heard the night before. I raise my voice, emphatic: "He didn't want any of this. How come this wasn't in the chart?" They look at each other, shrug—they have no clue. They ask me, "Who the was the nurse on last night?" I describe him, but they can't do anything in the moment, but will find out what happened. My rant is for me—surrogate for

Pete: "How come no one filled the Advanced Directives for him?" They all know this is standard upon admission, but it wasn't done. I felt guilty that I didn't take more time to fill it out myself. There was absolutely nothing anyone can do. I left the staff standing there and went into Pete's room afraid of something unknown.

Pete was totally sedated. I stood over him, agonized that here he was—things done to him that he was not wanting. My fault? The hospitals fault? Divine intervention? There were hurt feelings in me: I was totally disturbed and angry. At who? Why? My guilt; feeling guilty, almost to the deepest part of my being, but I remained prayerful. What came into my mind were two prayers—Sufi/Jewish prayers. "There is no Reality Except God. La Illaha Il Allah Hu; Sh'ma Yisrael." For some unknown reason, that was how it was intended. Pete was still alive. Maybe it was good not knowing anything else.

Leaving the hospital on unsteady feet I went to Arupa's house where we commiserated with each other. We put our souls together as we tried to be one with Pete remembering our promises to him. She appreciates that I know hospital work and will lead the effort to help work through what needs to be done.

That night back to see Pete, asking myself how was I going to deal with the nurse who heard Pete state his wishes the night before. There was an uneasiness I was feeling about confronting him. Then, before I know it, we see each other as he walks towards Pete's room. There's no waiting for him to say anything: but in a low, strained, hospital voice, I express anger, but don't like expressing anger. "What the hell happened? You heard him last night. I'm pissed."

"I'm pissed too." He stops my action, whatever that was going to be. He's pissed?

"Whaddya mean, you're pissed?"

He tells me: "I talked with Pete after you left. He told me the same thing that he told us together. I had a tech in with me so we had two witnesses. I paged the doctor a few times for him to come up and sign the order. He was busy on another emergency and never came up to sign the order. I knew this was going to happen if it didn't get signed."

What a story. It's like a movie script. Ten years living in Hollywood, my thoughts immediately create their own scenario. It was easy for me to trust what the nurse tells me, feeling his sincerity. An old friend, another male nurse is standing in another room. We knowingly stare at each other for a broken moment. This is real and here's Pete. An oversight. Sorry, but you're alive Pete. A drama is going to be played out and you're the main character.

The nurse and I spend time standing next to Pete, who is in a drugged state, unaware of all that's going on around him. The nurse is remorseful, but it was beyond him. I spend an hour standing at the foot of Pete's bed looking at him. I send him loving energy, unable to rationalize what wasn't done, having a hard time understanding why this is going on with Pete. Two days ago, in a tent in the woods, now this. A part of me feels something is out of harmony. I'm not sure what it is. Maybe nothing is. Maybe everything is as its intended. I try to understand my uneasy acceptance of the elements of life that are not easily understood. Damn, this is a hard one.

The next morning returning to the hospital a compassionate nurse tells me that Pete was awake when the doctor came to see him. "The doctor asked him two times if he wanted the breathing tube removed: he shook his head 'no.'" The nurse told me again, "We asked him a few times. He never changed his mind." Later when thinking about this, it occurs to me, that out of context, when one is not dying, signing a living will stating that one doesn't want heroic measures, is one thing, but once someone is hooked up to life support and they have to make the decision to end their own life, whew, it's looking into another frame of life where one has never been.

I can't stop asking myself about not being more attentive to the Advanced Directives. My mind: "What's the lesson? Pay more attention, or was this simply Pete's destiny and has nothing to do with me?" But it does because there is a feeling inside of me that feels something.

The hospital business for Pete went on for ten days. There were many talks with doctors, nurses and social workers. It was hard for me to deal with some of the medical drama, but having been a hospital social worker, I wove myself through being an attentive friend and advocate.

On the other hand, there was something in me that felt in control. Ever since I've been around dying people I found it to be my work. I responded to it many years previously and more recently working for three years in a nursing home. Now my work was with Pete. I don't want to sound like a mad man, but people die all the time and some of us are called to help along the way.

When Pete became somewhat alert on his second day,

I was able to joke with him a bit about his circumstance: "Pete, if we showed you a picture before we left the camp of what you would look like today, would you have come with us?" He gave me an expected hard shake of the head, "No." Not only is he hooked up to all the technology, but also his long beard is shaved off and his long hair shortened. I jokingly asked the staff what happened to the hair, but no one seemed to have taken responsibility for what was once an integral part of Pete.

For those first two days the most to be done for Pete, or for myself, was visit with him while he slept on morphine. I mainly stood at the foot of his bed praying and trying to ease his discomfort and again mine. I did a Buddhist meditation and prayer, tonglen, which is done for those who are dying or in distress. I try and take in all the dark that might be surrounding Pete; envisioning a black cloud of smoke into my own heart, sending back light for Pete's comfort. This was comfortable for me since in my meditations there is a practice of taking in light and sending it out to the world, sometimes into distressed places on the planet, now the distress was right in front of me.

In the discussions with the doctors they advised putting a tracheotomy tube in his trachea. I was able to have this discussion with the doctors while Pete was somewhat alert explaining to him he would be more comfortable then having the tube in his mouth and down his throat. I assured him the trach surgery was minimal. With a tube placed through a small opening to provide an airway and to remove secretions from the lungs. He agreed. He still trusts me. This was done the following day.

One doctor, his attending, the man in charge, (we remembered each other from when I was a social worker at the hospital) gave me good advise, suggesting we do things step by step. The next step was to take out the nasal gastric tube and put a feeding tube directly into his stomach.

By the fourth day Pete was completely restrained, from first his wrists, to now, arms, legs, shoulders with a posy chest restraint. This was all done because he was constantly pulling the nasal gastric tube out of his nose, irritating his throat even more. No amount of pleading by the nurses or myself was able to stop his annoyance of the nasal gastric tube. Previously, mostly restrained, he managed to wiggle his body into a position to pull out the tube, until finally he was totally restrained. My friend, who lived in the woods, on his own, no constraints, drinking beer and smoking cigarettes now this is how I see him, How does he feel? In those moments I could only know my part.

We talked about the gastric feeding tube, me explaining it to him so he understood the procedure. Since he now wanted to live I told him this would work and he wouldn't have to remain in the hospital. "Pete, I can get you into a nursing home where I worked for three years as the social worker. Maybe you can even have a beer or two a day. This was the policy they allowed in the past." Naturally he agreed to the feeding tube procedure. With his finger over the hole, he gurgled, asking me, "What's going to happen to me?"

"Pete, we don't know. I'm sorry you're going through all this. It all could have been over for you if the hospital followed procedures, but people are people. You know. They screw up. So for now you're still here. I know you'll feel better in the nursing home."

"Will I get better?" He quietly gurgled?

With sadness in my voice—how else could I feel? "We don't know Pete. We just don't know."

After the gastric tube was placed in him he was in a bit of pain for the next two days, but was helped with morphine.

A day or so later, he was discharged from the medical intensive care unit to a regular room. He was now feeling much better, more at ease. He was able to talk a bit by putting his finger over the hole of the trach. What was annoying was the constant drip of mucous from the hole, slopping down his chest. He was reminded to wipe it, but wiped his nose, thinking it was coming out of there, but soon, he sort of got the hang of things.

Seeing him stabilized, my talks began with the social worker at the hospital to get him discharged to the nursing home. The social worker remembered me from many years back through her husband who was the brother to a favorite client of mine at a mental health center. It was a bit relieving to work with friendly, like mined people. Everyone has been saint-like. I told the social worker that I called hospice and they would take the referral when he was in the nursing home. She said she'd take care of the discharge to the nursing home.

Because his throat cancer was now the issue to deal with the doctors unrealistically suggested radiation and chemotherapy. That's what they do to try and save lives. It was obvious to me that in his fragile condition, this would weaken him more than his body would be able to handle. One nurse even confided to me, a bit bluntly, "it would probably kill him."

"Pete, the docs are suggesting they do radiation or chemo on the cancer in your throat."

He was adamant, shaking his head and gurgling, "No, no, I don't want that." Then Pete told me as clearly as he could he wasn't going for it even before I brought it up.

He was admitted to the nursing home. Rather than have him transported by ambulance, I drove him to the nursing home myself. It was the closest one to where most of his friends lived in case they wanted to visit. Fortunately some of the staff still knew me, which meant added attention for his care. That was a big plus in this nursing home. When I was there, it had the worst reputation in our community. There was new ownership now and my favorite nurse had returned after taking another job. She assured me that things were better. Pete was going to get the care he needed.

Odd how all this was playing out. He might have been dead if not for the mistake by hospital staff, and myself. So, again, this is how the Universe, the nature of things, worked out a plan for Pete to have more time on this earth. We were just going to have to wait for how much time that would be.

When he was admitted to the nursing home, I went a bit ballistic talking with staff known and unknown to me. I needed to give them information about Pete's previous life style and the care I thought he needed. Annoying the doctor while she was busy was contrary to my professional judgment, but I needed to make sure she knew his situation; even calling her a few times until she told me to stop calling. When she finally did see him she wrote orders for morphine, as needed, beer if requested. Maybe being a pain in the ass helped with the orders.

The next day, four of us came to see visit Pete. Arupa and Pat from the Home Van, and Valerie a friend of mine who does Reiki healing. Reiki is energy healing similar to laying on of hands, but with special training so the practitioner directs "life force" healing energy through their hands to the patient. Valerie also brought fresh carrot and beet juice for Pete. When he drank it, there was quite a scene as it squirted out of his trach tube. The red juice ran down his chest and onto the floor causing the staff to panic a bit. They thought he was bleeding from the throat. We had a bit of a chuckle, as we eased their concern.

As we sat talking with Pete he began to complain of lower back pain. Valerie began to work on him, but he brushed her away throwing a pillow on the ground. Then he crawled to the floor as we watched questioning what he was doing. We quickly realized he knew exactly what he wanted: to be prone on the floor and more comfortable. Valerie continued to work on him while he rested on the ground. Not the usual nursing home procedures.

Pete stabilized a bit more in the home, becoming strong enough to use a wheel chair. He was able to roll himself onto the outdoor-screened patio for an occasional cigarette. We brought beer for him, but with the morphine, he seemed to have lost his taste. He wasn't even smoking so much. The hospice social worker who I knew for many years, assured me he was doing as fine as he could considering he probably had cancer throughout his throat and torso.

Pete was in the nursing home for a couple of weeks before getting back his famous smile, but yet, getting thinner and weaker. His legs and arms looked like twigs. He told me he was drinking the Ensure, but I didn't ask anyone since it didn't make much difference. He laughed when we talked about how he tricked us in the woods telling us he was drinking the Ensure we brought out to him. In truth he was putting it in his storage tent. He told me he didn't want us to feel bad that he didn't like it so he just stored it. When we eventually cleaned out his camp, we gave all he saved to other homeless people we knew who could use it.

I saw him every other day, spending about half an hour or so sitting on his bed talking. He wasn't going outside much, satisfied with the bed—the morphine. Pete never was a drug user, but made the most of the morphine, admitting, "I don't want the pain." I assured him it was the right thing. "You had enough pain in this life." He smiled nodding his head.

His trach tube was constantly dripping mucous he wiped, coughed up, acting annoyed. He shook his head angrily, acting the same way when his papers and cards wouldn't go in his wallet easily, or his night table drawer wouldn't open.

He didn't have too much longer to be with us, but who knew how long that would be.

I felt it was time to ask him, "Pete, it's not easy to ask you, but what do you want done with your body—cremation or burial?"

"Cremation," he gurgled.

"And your remains, should we spread them around your camp?" As I was having this talk, it all felt awkward, maybe a bit contrived, because something in me felt none of it made any difference to Pete. But he never gave me that information, so I felt compelled to go through the motions.

"No! No memories." He raised his hands in the air, giving the impression he just wanted to go up in smoke and that was fine.

"Should I just leave your remains with the mortuary?" He shrugged.

When I asked him about his thoughts on what's next, he shrugged again, "When we go, were just gone," he rasped.

Because there were no relatives we were able to contact he had to sign a document that cremation is what he wanted. I had previously gone through something similar with another man who died in the woods and the County Social Services wouldn't do a cremation without family consent. That man had a girlfriend who cared for him to the end, but she wasn't family. The mortuary refused to do a cremation.

To help Pete, I called the social worker from hospice who said she'd have a document made up for Pete to sign that'll have places for witnesses. Hopefully that will satisfy the bureaucracy. In the past there were uncomfortable incidents when family would show up after the cremation, wanting to know where their family member was buried.

In the evening I brought him some cheap wine he requested in the morning, MD 20 20. Mad Dog? I had no clue. He still had a barely sipped beer on his nightstand. I stood praying by his bed that evening, which I hadn't done in a while. I felt he was getting close. His weight was probably 75 pounds. Amazing, living on that thin thread of life's energy still coming through to him; enough though to keep him going.

Arupa at times, jokingly, but in all seriousness, referred to Pete as being a sacred being, a Sadhu, which is a Hindu term for one who renounces the things of the world. He certainly did that living as he did in the woods. We really don't know who any of us have been, or where our spirits have come from as we work on trying to know who we are in this life and where we might be going. For Pete though, in this life, all that mystical business was a none-issue. He was grounded in the here and now, day to day living—beer and cigarettes, occasional food.

Pete was always so appreciative, thanking me when I came by and sat on his bed. That was his nature, always appreciating what we did when he needed things living in the woods. But now, his time was getting closer and it was my honor to be with him.

Two mornings after the signing of the cremation I had a phone call from a nurse at the nursing home. She had to tell me he pulled out the trac tube. My friend Minnie, a saint of a nurse, got on the phone and told me, "Sh'mal, you should come in." When I worked there, Minnie and I became good friends. She got to know me so well that when she felt some one was close to dying, but wasn't able to let go, she would ask me to go talk, or just be with them.

That morning with Pete, his last, I watched him twist and turn, maneuver his body into any position that might make him comfortable. No position worked.

Earlier that morning in doing my meditation practice, before the phone call, I felt it was important for me to spend more time sitting, paying attention to my breath, focus my tonglen practice on Pete with a bit more concentration and intention. A deep part of me knew I would soon be offering help.

"Pete, it's getting close. Try and relax, get comfortable. It's all going to be okay; have a sip of beer," which he took with a straw, but with barely any strength to even sip. We held the can together—he took out the straw—then with both hands wrapped around mine, he tried sipping, as it spilled down his chest. I had a towel near by and cleaned it up, as he pushed the beer away into my hands. I felt odd, giving someone beer as possibly their last liquid. I was a bit bothered I didn't offer water. He loved beer.

I called out to a nurse passing his room asking her, "When does Pete get his morphine?" A few minutes later she brought him what he needed. It did little good though as he continued to shift and turn looking for a comfortable position. All morning staff who found him a likable resident, came in and out of his room, stood near by, being with him. Some talked with me, remembering when I worked there. One resident came in to relate a complimentary story she heard about me. I didn't want to feel flattered since this was my life work.

I looked for words that might help. "Close your eyes Pete. You can get ready and when you go, go to the light. It's all I know Pete, what I heard about the next plane. Go to the light." He'd close his eyes for a few seconds—opened them. It was agony for him trying to get comfortable.

"It's close Pete."

He waved, like a good-bye. I've never known that kind of good-bye. I knew in that moment, it was a wave I'd never forget. It was Pete. He knew it was getting that close. Nurses and aides came in to fix his sheets, adjust the back of the bed so he could sit up. I rearranged a pillow behind his back. Nothing was making much difference. There was no comfort before dying if one hasn't prepared.

I thought of the struggle some of the nursing home residents went through when I worked right there and the "frightened to death" expressions on their faces when they were gone. It was much different for those who were more or less at peace with themselves having some sense what they believed was coming next. Whether what they believed was coming, came or not, didn't make any difference, except it helped make their leaving easier.

After a couple of hours I went home and ate, took a nap, read from the "Tibetan Book of Living and Dying," the section on tonglen. I visualized Pete, where he was, what he was going through, what is known to me and what wasn't known.

I was gone for three hours. When I returned, he had passed from here; his body was lying inert. I rubbed the top of his head, trying to help his spirit leave through the crown charka. Did prayers for him that he was comfortable; at peace; that he needn't return looking for more beer and cigarettes, hopefully having had his fill in this lifetime.

I'm always in wonderment how when we take on one

good thing to do, we never know where it's going to bring us; what effect it's going to have on our life or the life of another. The interbeingness of the Buddhist philosophy is incorporated into my life because I feel it in me, what Buddha taught. Similarly, in reading what the Sufis have to say, especially about life and the importance of breath. And what Judaism, my birth religion has to say about the mystical path of this life and the four worlds we inhabit while here. I am trying to somehow make my path in harmony with all paths, especially when a friend who is at the end of this path going on to endless distances beyond our knowing. I am thankful for this gift of life and what is learned.

# The Legacy of Rose Pearl

Rose Pearl made a phone call to me reaching out to tell me she was dying. She made it clear it wouldn't be that very moment, but in the near future. Rose said she was calling because she needed some one to take care of her affairs after she passed on. Until that moment, we didn't know each other and had never met. What I do know is that phone call, from a "stranger," had a strong impact on my life.

Rose told me she found my name in the *Barter Network Newsletter* in our town. The BNN had been around for a couple of years, but I hadn't known what to put in as my specialty to share in exchange with the community. I finally decided to share my experience and expertise in working with the elderly, the sick and the dying.

By putting out work I knew well, what was my most sacred part, some one came into my life who had the most to give. After her introduction, Rose told me a bit more about who she was then she asked me about myself. I told her, "I'm the Director of Social Services for a nursing home and I've worked with elders for 20 years." As I heard myself tell her this, my thoughts briefly questioned what she told me. Was this Rose some one who was mentally stable? Did she really have no one else to help her? Her voice though was soft and confident. This enabled me, for the moment, to trust what she was telling me—odd though, to discuss her dying with a complete stranger.

She went on to tell me she was 82 years old and had moved to Florida a few years ago to marry a 40 year-old black man who was a lifer in the worst prison in Florida. Rose said they met through the mail. She said, "I began corresponding with prisoners when I became slightly disabled due to arthritis in my legs."

I had to ask her to repeat their ages, so I was clear about what she said. She repeated their ages. I cautioned myself again about how sane this woman was. My doubts quickly dissolved when she told me she had studied the works of Rudolph Steiner for fifty years. Steiner was the founder of Anthroposophy. This is a philosophy that postulates the existence of an objective, intellectually comprehensible spiritual world accessible to direct experience through inner development. This philosophy earned him a reputation as one of the deepest, most profound thinkers of our time. There are primary and secondary schools, in many countries, Waldorf Schools, that espouse his teachings. I was somewhat familiar with his teachings. Rose told me, "I have a whole library of his books and need to make plans for them when I die. I have two nieces who aren't interested in any of my things, but are emotionally close to me. They live in Chicago and we don't see each other often."

As she told me all this, a fascination was gained in me about this "Rose."

Because I worked in a nursing home I had been close to many dying people. In those moments her voice was so clear and upbeat it didn't sound like someone who was dying soon. I hesitated a bit, then, in a gentle and kind voice, "You don't sound like you are dying."

There was a pause, she laughed, as she told me, "My niece in Chicago tells me I've been saying that for ten years." I pursued it a bit more, "So are you dying soon?" She said, "I believe my time is getting close, but for now I'd like to meet you and get to know you better. Would you come and visit me?"

I was still a bit uncertain about making a visit to her, but also felt adventurous to go and meet Rose. The unexpected in life has always been tempting to me. She gave me directions and I made the 30 minute drive a few days later. Rose came to the door in a wheelchair, but immediately excused herself and climbed into a hospital bed explaining, "I'm so much more comfortable in bed since my legs bother me from arthritis." Rose was a plump, cherub like woman, who lived in a small, subsidized apartment—two rooms, kitchenette and bathroom.

When she was back in the bed she wrapped a soft, white, shawl around her shoulders and made herself comfortable. She looked at me directly, smiled broadly, and made herself known to me with little ambiguity in what she said.

Right away I appreciated the easy way she spoke.

"I moved here to be closer to my husband Sylvester. We were writing to each other for five years and something special transpired between us. We fell in love and decided to get married. It's difficult living so close to him though and not being able to visit."

Rose told me she lived simply. "I don't have much finances. I receive some help, food and personal care from an agency that serves the elderly." She said she wasn't eating much any more, living on vegetarian foods for decades and now mostly Ensure. I appreciated sharing with her my long time vegetarian diet. We spent about two hours talking together, me mostly listening to her talk about her life as a Waldorf teacher, weaver, bookstore owner, traveler, wife three times over, before marrying Sylvester. She was so honest and pure in her conversation. There was no need for me to judge her for following her heart and spirit in marrying this man who was so totally different, on the physical plane, than she was.

She told me again that she met Sylvester through the mail. She said, "I answered an ad in the *Sojourner Magazine*, for prisoners seeking pen pals. After my arthritis progressed, I couldn't get out and be active in a community. I needed something worthwhile to do, so I began corresponding with prisoners." Rose showed me a copy of the book, *"Doing Time Together,"* a published version of the first two years of the letters she and Sylvester wrote to each other. "We didn't make much money from the book, but it did get some notoriety due to the uniqueness of our coming together and our subsequent marriage."

Rose eventually talked about the ongoing problems Sylvester had in prison. She shared with me, with a bit of tears in her eyes, the brutality he and others encountered. Because of her letter writing to the warden of the prison, to state prison officials and newspapers complaining about the brutality in prisons and advocating for prison reform she was barred from seeing her husband. Sylvester, for one reason or another, was in and out of solitary confinement. Rose gave me the book to take home, her last copy, which was a revealing book about prison life and the spiritual transformation Sylvester experienced.

A week after my visit I received a letter from Rose. She gave me instructions on what she wanted me to do with her meager possessions. Her letter had the names and addresses of everyone I needed to contact. It also stated her wishes for treatment or actually non-treatment, if she was close to dying.

It was odd to get such a serious letter from someone I barely knew. I called her and asked, "Rose, aren't you jumping ahead a bit about your death being so imminent?" She laughed, "I feel it's close and I need to cover all my bases."

It felt a bit awkward being asked to take on the life possessions and work of this new friend. But since God had plucked me out, choose me to be Rose's friend and aide, who was I to question this course of life.

In reading the book of the letters between her and Sylvester, there was a letter Rose wrote in early June 1989. Rose gave her husband assurance to not worry about her dying soon. "I have about 10 more years," she told him. Rose contacted me in early May of 1999. She died a month later on June 2.

On May 23 Rose had a near fatal stroke leaving her almost totally paralyzed. Our one mutual friend, notified me of Rose's stroke. I went to see Rose who was in the

intensive care unit of a local hospital. She was hooked up
to life support. She had struggled so much against these
encumbrances, tubes in tubes out, the staff strapped her
arms to the bed rails. With a dear friend of mine, Eleanor,
we stood helplessly by the bed compassionately looking at
Rose. In her letter to me she indicated she did not want
life support. It was up to me to do something to free her of
hospital technologies. I didn't have long to wait. A hospice
nurse I had just met that week in the nursing home, as if
called by me, showed up to see a patient of his in the ICU.
I wasted no time telling him about Rose and her wishes
to die without feeding tube, oxygen, or I.V. liquids. I
wasn't family, but had the letter Rose sent me with wishes
for non-treatment and the name and phone number of
Rose's niece in Chicago. The nurse wasted no time and
called Rose's niece who confirmed her aunt's wishes. By
grace, there was an empty bed at the Hospice House,
and that same day Rose was moved. All this seemed too
synchronistic to be coincidental. Another indication to me
of how the universe works.

I had put my ad in the *Barter Network Newsletter*
to offer this help, but events seemed to be happening
as if by script. It felt like something else was going on.
I asked myself, "Is there something I'm to learn from
knowing Rose?" It came to me one night, standing by
her bed in Hospice House, searching myself for what
exactly to say to Rose. Much of the time I simply stood
near her and smiled, held her hand, kept her company. At
times though, there was the need in me to talk with her.
She never spoke after the stroke, but her open eyes kept
shining while her mouth had an occasional smile.

What also was very special is that when she was awake she kept her left arm in constant motion. Amazingly, as she lay in bed, mostly paralyzed, she was able to keep her arm raised in the air along side her head, moving it around in circles. It was as if to let all those around her know she was still with us. As she looked up at me, in her eyes I felt her asking: "Why is this happening?"

"Rose, you just have to wait your turn; there's a long line ahead of you and it's going slow." Even with all those I helped at this stage in the nursing home, this thought never came to me, but it seemed an appropriate assessment. Bombs were dropping in Kosovo, children were shooting children in Columbine High School in Colorado; she had to wait.

It came to me that in Rose's dying dance, for those ten days, my whole purpose in meeting her, was to help her through this period in her life. And for me to understand—to be even less fearful of death. For ten days she was only partially there. She dozed off regularly, but when awake she knew I was with her. She didn't go the way she planned: that deep, middle of night kind of death. I had the sense she appreciated my presence in being with her and again—purpose and synchronicity: "This is why I put in the ad; this is why she called me."

As with other dying people I mostly prayed, audibly and in silence, for her to be at peace. I was passing on the same feeling of peacefulness she spent most of her life radiating to others. It wasn't hard or easy being close to death with a special person—it just was a gift to be present. And for her part, it truly felt she was being a good sport, knowing God prepared her well for this time.

All along I was appreciating this opportunity given to me by Rose—being plucked out of my day to day to be with her as she waited patiently for her last breath.

On her last night, her breathing became labored, alternating between 30 seconds of slow breathing and increasing into a heavy breathing, then decreasing back to the slow quiet breathing, almost stopping. I could feel she was getting within hours or minutes of her last breath. I left at 10:00 p.m. and she took her last breaths at 2:00 a.m.

After Rose passed on, I spent many days and nights going through some of the boxes of copied letters to Sylvester. She was so tender, as she expressed her love to him. Rose was teaching him a new way to see life. His letters were always thankful that she was in his life with her special love for him. He also was very graphic in depicting life in infamous Florida State Prison. Sylvester had spent most of his adult life in and out of prison and was now in for life for an almost fatal assault on a sadistic prison guard who had previously beaten Sylvester mercilessly.

In the letters she wrote and received from many prisoners, Rose expressed empathy for the cruelty prisoners were subjected to in most prisons. She also felt conflict knowing they had been perpetrators themselves. She wrote though about her global understanding, that many had been victims as children, taking it out on others and consequently, suffering societies punishment.

Rose had not come from a cloistered world by any means, but her life never knowingly connected with criminals. Then, turning 70, unable to do all her favorite activities anymore, she looked into the world, way outside anything she had known before. She chose to write to those who were the least socially acceptable in America. They are the lepers of our time. Maybe she took the lead from St. Francis who chose to work with lepers because none else would.

She had books of many great humanitarians: Christ, her Teacher, The Peace Pilgrim, Albert Schweitzer, Gandhi, Rudolf Steiner and other great or common seekers on the peace path. Her collection of letters, books and notes are filled with pictures of angels and saints, confirming her belief in the sacredness of all life.

After Rose left this plane, I began a correspondence with Sylvester. My first letters were about the brief time I knew Rose and how thankful I was for her being in my life. In all honesty, his letters were emotionally hard for me to read. They contained too many graphic details of life inside Florida State Prison. At some point our letter writing ended.

# A Brother Is Sick

"I don't want any home-care nurse coming out to see me." These were the words, Jeffrey, a patient, told the home care nurse who saw him on a home visit she made after a doctor wrote an order. The nurse gave me the referral, and asked me to make a courtesy social work visit. She felt he and his brother needed some assistance. There were going to be a lot of issues to deal with on my home visit to this man. The nurse told me that Jeffrey had AIDS, cancer, and syphilis. Because he was refusing nursing care he wasn't going to be a home care patient. I was allowed to make one visit to see what council I could give.

Before going to their house I took some time for myself by pulling off the rural road where there was a metal gate blocking the entrance to a path leading into a small forest area.

I climbed over the gate and walked into the pine forest. A sign designated the area as a bird sanctuary with a painting of a woodpecker. I walked along the path consciously paying attention to my breath—breathing in, breathing out; breathe in and walk breathe out and walk. Breath work is a part of my daily meditation-yoga practice. After a short while I stopped and looked further into the forest, breathed some more, and walked on. I have no expectation in doing this meditation practice, just being present and breathing. I do this personal work because it feels good to me. It feels right. It helps me be in touch with nature with the natural rhythm of my life. These walks, or just sitting in nature, give me something not so available in my daily schedule. I spend a lot of time in buildings; one is an extremely large hospital the others are medical clinics. They are mostly devoid of outside nature, except for a few plants which do very little to ease the pervasive medical environment. My true home is in a natural setting. It is helpful for me to be fed by nature. Sometimes being with other people brings a similar fulfillment.

Today, something in me felt it was important to be fed before going to see Jeffrey and his brother, Albert, who helps to take care of him. I need sustenance because sometimes when making home calls to people with illnesses, there is a lot of myself that I have to give. I can give and hopefully they can receive. I have to admit, though, there is some feeding back to me in making these visits.

Let me be clear: I don't exactly get fed from the patient directly, but something comes to me from the transpersonal interaction we share. Maybe it's a fair trade. When I give, I receive. It's love: a universal principal. Biblical. The love is what I'm trying to transmit.

My belief: All life is always giving to us if we remain open. For me, taking a short walk in the woods allows the natural energy, energy from creation, to join me: My feet touch the earth, my skin is touched by the air and tree energy that surrounds me. Then something in me feels better able to deal with the lives of patients who are frequently having a difficult time. And ultimately, my deeper self, is better able to deal with my own life and this work I've been given to do.

After staying long enough to feel ready it was time to walk out of the forest with a hope Jeffrey and his brother Albert would be at home. A few days earlier they weren't at home even though I had called and told Albert's girlfriend, Annie, I'd be by. Yesterday I left a message on the answering machine I would be there in the morning. It was just taking a chance they would be home since no one called back. Annie was very concerned about what was going on with Jeffrey. Neither she, nor Albert knew for sure how sick Jeffrey was. She had asked me to find out what his diagnosis was—to try to get him tested for AIDS. Albert had a couple of kids he'd like to see on the weekends, but with his brother there, possibly with AIDS, he was hesitant to have the kids around. I told her, "No one can force Jeffery to do anything he doesn't want to do. I'll see if I can help."

They lived in a small wood framed house in a part of town where I felt it wouldn't be safe on the street at night. Albert, the healthy brother, answered the door and said his brother would be right out. Jeffrey came out and shook my hand. Barely. His handshake was the kind that always bothered me—very limp, barely any shake at all, with no eye contact; his face down to the floor. I wasn't sure if it was because he didn't want to meet with a white man, or if he had no self-esteem, or if he was just weak. After our brief introduction, he turned around and went back into the room he came out from. He closed the door leaving me with his brother.

Since I knew there was tension in the house between the brothers, I did my best to ease into the conversation with Albert. Our talk didn't get too far before Jeffrey slowly walked back out of the room. He sat on a chair that was not close to his brother or me. He didn't say a word.

My intention was to try and connect with both of them so they would trust me and talk about what was going on. "Jeffrey, the nurse who saw you last week asked me to come out and talk with the two of you because of troubles you and your brother are having." I paused and waited.

Jeffrey began to talk, very softly. He appeared, passive, docile, like his handshake. "I came here because I have no where else to go, Mr. Bob. I'm real sick and to be honest, I'm not sure if I have AIDS or what. I don't want to be here, but I have no place to go. I know my brother is angry at me, but what can I do?"

After he spoke for a few minutes Albert jumped in on the conversation. He needed to make his point about what he thought was going on between them. There was the feeling right off he was waiting for an opportunity to tell someone about his dilemma. It felt like Jeffrey, though, had more to share.

As Albert began to talk I interrupted him, "Albert, it sounded like your brother had more to say. Why don't you," but he interrupted me too.

"No, Mr. Bob, let me tell you something. He lied

to me. Flat out. Lied." He spoke in a raised voice, not loud, but he was going to make sure I heard what he had to say. "He never told me he had cancer when I brought him home from the hospital. And I don't know about the other either. He won't say anything about that." He sounded irritated, annoyed and discouraged. It was easy to hear the anger in his voice. I looked at Jeffrey who began to mumble, not making a clear response to his brother's accusation. He mumbled on until Albert said, "See, he's not saying anything even now." It felt like there was a wide gap between them.

It was imperative for me be careful with the two brothers and not create more tension and distrust between them. It was also important to draw Jeffrey out a bit; to have more information about what was going on with him, also, between them. Jeffrey though preferred to talk about the trouble he had keeping his sores clean.

"I need patches and the cleaning stuff. I can do it all myself. I don't need no nurse but I'm running out of gauze pads."

"Getting the gauze pads won't be a problem Jeffrey, but what's going on with the two of you living together?"

"I'm just here," he said in a sullen, no affect voice. He had little to say about anything going on in the house, except, "This is my brother's house. He threw me out two times already. What am I supposed to do or think about with him doing that? I'm a real sick man."

"What are you supposed to do? What am I supposed to do?" Albert responded, again in a slightly, irritated, raised voice. "I don't even know what you got? I had to go all the way into town to the hospital to talk with the doctors to find out you had cancer. And you still won't get that test. One day he tells me he has it. Then the next day he tells me he doesn't. I don't know shit and he's living in my house."

"When we were younger," Albert continued, "we spent more time together, but now, he's, 42, and I'm 37 and we haven't spent much time together for 10 years. I've lived in town for the past few years and Jeffrey comes and stays here for a few months at a time."

Jeffery passively sat and listened, then said, "Look here, Mr. Bob, we didn't get along okay before my illness, but now, I'm being honest, and I'm really uptight over what's happening."

Albert seemed like he was doing his best to keep it together. "I'll tell you something Mr. Bob. If my brother isn't going to be straight with me, I'll take him back to where he was living before I went and got him. I can do that. You know I will," he said, pointing his finger at Jeffrey. "I will too. I can't keep living this way. You got those oozing, bloody sores on your body and you throw away the gauze pads and shit in the bathroom trash. I want my kids here and I can't bring them here if you got that other and...and with that blood and shit. Fuck it man. Excuse me Mr. Bob, but I don't feel right about this."

"Jeffrey," I began, looking at him directly, "why don't you get tested for AIDS? Your brother will feel better if he knows."

He didn't say anything. He just sat, not looking at either Albert or me.

"See. See that shit. That's what I'm talking about. And he's my big brother. He's been getting his way with me ever since we were kids and he keeps treating me like I'm bad in my house. Him wanting to do what he wants to do and not caring what he puts me through."

"Hey Mr. Bob," Jeffrey finally spoke, "he's my brother and I don't want him to get sick from me." There were tears in his voice that was low, even lower than before. I had to strain a bit to hear, even though he was only a few feet away from me. "I'm the one who's going through all of this. I got to do what feels right for me. He doesn't understand that. He only thinks about what he's going through. Yea, I got the one thing and I'm scared of it. Maybe I have the other. I really don't know what to do. I've been trying to lead a good life. Not messing with a whole lot of women. No drugs. One girl for the past three years. Maybe I got it from her. I don't know. It's all tearing me up inside. Do this. Do that. Go here for this test; go there for another. Talk to this one; wait on the phone; get passed on to some one else. It's been driving me crazy. No money. I can't work. Not sure where I'm going to get treatments. Who's going to pay for me to get help? I need a lot of help and can't do much for myself."

I looked over to Albert, waiting to hear his response. He didn't seem to know what to say. There was an uncomfortable silence. I wasn't sure if the pause was good or not. It was touchy being there. How much can I do to make things better for them? It felt like I clicked with them quickly considering everything. But I knew my visit with them wasn't going to straighten much out in our short time together. Besides the words, the energy of discomfort going on between them felt pervasive. They each had their own take on the situation.

Jeffery had cancer around his groin. The nurse told me it metastasized; now he had it on his penis, abdomen, and hip. The worst the doctors wanted to do was cut it all away, leaving only part of a man. The least intrusive treatment was radiation. Earlier, when Albert left the room for a short while, I discussed with Jeffrey the options the hospital had presented for treatment.

"Mr. Bob, I don't know what to do. You know what I got. It ain't good and maybe it's never going to get better." I could hear the pain and hurt in his voice. It felt like it was in his total being; from a depth no one could ever feel.

The silence was felt. It hung there, surrounding the two of them: Actually the three of us. Their tension made me feel a bit uncomfortable. What were the right words to help them work through this? I hesitated for a few moments thinking how to proceed. Finally letting go of trying to think of words, "Albert, your brother is going through something that we can't even imagine. You're his brother. Look man, you're feeling this more than any one can. The nurse asked me to come by to try to help him as the patient and you as his brother. You have a big decision. How do you make the right decisions—to be fair to yourself and your children? To be right to him?" I tried to watch myself, not wanting to sound preachy, offering a bit of council in this brief time. Ultimately it would be left to the two of them and to life's will to come through in the end.

Albert stood up. He was much taller than his older brother. Strong and handsome; he appeared to be a hard worker. It was easy to sense he wasn't sure how to continue. There was anger still hanging on to him. It would not go away quickly, unless the illness moved fast.

"But he lied to me. Just lied," Albert finally said. "And what am I supposed to do about that? Just forget it all and let him go about doing what he wants." He paused for a bit and walked over to a window. He stood a few moments. Just looking out. He turned around. "Shit. I live here." His voice was raised. "I don't want to get nothing. He can be careful, but we read it in the papers all the time. This happens, that happens, and soon, someone else got it. He has to find out what he got. Then we can go from there." He stopped talking, turned and looked out the window. Longer this time. "I'll tell both of you. I'm glad the nurse sent you out, Mr. Bob, so you can hear me too. Tell the nurse what I'm saying: If he won't do that, get tested, then I can take him some place else." He stopped. Looked from me to his brother.

"Jeffrey," Albert said in a softer voice, "don't you want to know for sure? Shit, we both know people with it. It's scary. We've seen it. But at least if I know, then I can deal with that. He can stay here—he's my bother, but I want to know what I'm dealing with. Yeah, you're right Jeffrey, I am thinking of myself. I'm thinking of you too, otherwise you wouldn't even be here. I gotta think of my kids and then you. You hear me? Find out what you got, then we can deal." Albert finished. Those were his last words. He walked off into the kitchen. Jeffrey just sat there looking at the floor.

I waited a few beats, "You hear him Jeffrey. It sounds like it has to be your move. Shit, it's easy for me to get you gauze pads and medical supplies. You got more on you than I want to see on any man. No one can tell you how to deal with it. You have to look inside of yourself and figure it out on your own. You say you have the Bible and that gives you peace. Look in it, meditate on what's going on, and see what answers come to you. I'll get in touch with you tomorrow and see about bringing you some supplies."

"Alright Mr. Bob. Thanks," but again, Jeffrey didn't look up from the floor. He just sat there.

I opened and closed the door myself; walked away and went back to the woods. I wanted to see a woodpecker before going back to the office, but none showed itself.

# About the Author

The stories in this book are about the work of helping people with their transition from this life to the next stage of existence. Although, the author has spent most of his work life as a community based social worker, in his early 40s, together with his ex-wife, they began to care for elders and partially disabled people in their home. This experience of caring for people at home was a lead-in for him to work as a social worker for a home care agency and later in a nursing home. In both of these employments he came in contact with many people in the end stage of their lives.

Like many people who experience spiritual transformations, after reading a number of spiritual books and practicing meditation and yoga, he began to feel he was on a spiritual path. One particular book, The Tibetan Book of Living and Dying, fascinated him. After reading it once, and then immediately a second time, he began to question whether there was something in his nature calling him to work with dying people.

Each of the nine stories in this book comes from a different circumstance in his life. The first two stories are about his mother and father. Although neither story is about their dying, but rather the care he gave to them preceding their death. All the other stories are about the intimate relationships the author developed, each in a different way, helping the dying person.

It's been impossible for the author to know why this work came into his life. All he knows for sure is that after reading the Tibetan Book of Living and Dying he was soon hired in a nursing home as the Director of Social Services. It was there that something in him felt moved, almost like being pulled, to be with many as they neared death. He has total gratitude about the gift of doing this work.

The author has five children and two stepchildren. Along with three of his own children, he has witnessed eight homebirths. Not many lay people have had this experience. There is a bit of wonderment about what it is in his life to have experienced those births and many deaths? One 52 year-old daughter came into his life in 2013 after not knowing each other. Yes, social networking has positive value. They are both appreciating the new connection.

He lives in Palm Coast, Florida with his life partner, Linda Solomon, a well know artist in many cities on the North East coast of Florida.

The author's 40 years as a social worker includes working with pre-school children, severely emotional disturbed children, mental health patients, at-risk teens and in a hospital.

While working with homeless people in Gainesville, Florida a video documentary was made about the work he was doing being a case manager for 15 mentally ill homeless people. It's called A Sh'mal World. In his 23 years living in Gainesville he also had many essays on social and political issues published in the Gainesville Sun.

Social work helped make him an activist for humane

issues and in 1982 during the Nuclear Weapon's Freeze he gave a speech in support of the Freeze before to the House of Representatives Subcommittee on Defense Appropriations.

As a young man, in 1970, the author left Los Angeles where had lived for 10 years and went to Santa Fe, New Mexico where the "hippie" revolution was in full swing. Although having just turned 30 and considered "not to be trusted" by the younger generation, he felt he was part of this movement. Having previously worked with the Head Start program in Los Angeles, he was hired to teach at the Santa Fe Community School, an alternative K thru 12 school. He and other teachers who had recently moved to Santa Fe formed a collective buying 40 acres in the Ozarks in northern Arkansas. He lived there for two years, "primitively," with no running water, only pump over a spring box, and no electricity, using candles and kerosene for light. He knows that living with nature was the perfect environment for the beginning of a spiritual transformation that has continued on. It was also in the Ozarks where he learned organic gardening and currently has a productive 40 x 30 foot vegetable garden.